NAVIGATING COURAGE

LEADING BEYOND FEAR

ROBIN MARTIN

NAVIGATING COURAGE

The Library of Congress has cataloged this book under the following: Martin, Robin Navigating Courage: Leading Beyond Fear / by Robin Martin
Library of Congress Control Number: 2019930114

ISBN 978-1-944581-14-5 (pbk)
ISBN-13: 978-1729642320 (CreateSpace Assigned)

Dedication

This book is dedicated to my mother, Gladys Priscilla Martin. Thank you for allowing me to live a free life to choose my path, learn from my mistakes and own my excellence. Thank you for fostering an environment where my voice was heard, my questions were valid and my "sass" was both honored and tempered when needed. The truth is, I have never accomplished any meaningful task without your guidance and love. All of my life's successes are wrapped in the protection of your prayers and love. I thank God that he gave you the strength to give me birth, the wisdom to guide my steps and, more importantly, the courage to let me be me. All mothers give birth; you gave me Freedom.

Contents

Dedication v

Preface ix

Introduction xi

PART 1

BIRD'S-EYE VIEW: DEFINE AND NAVIGATE

Chapter 1 Define: In Search of My Mother's Gardens 1

Chapter 2 Navigate: Fill the Room and Know Your Name 13

Chapter 3 Discover: In the Storm 25

PART 2

EQUITY: RACE, GENDER AND ATHLETICS

Chapter 4 Race: The 1 Percent Club 39

Chapter 5 Gender: Internal/External Consequences 49

Chapter 6 Athletics: Too Much for Their Too Little 59

PART 3

DIVERSITY, INCLUSION AND HIGHER EDUCATION

Chapter 7 Diversity: Upward Trajectory Upended 75

Chapter 8 Included--The World is Collapsing, and So am I .. 85

Chapter 9 Institutional Diversity Gets an F 97

PART 4

LEADERSHIP MATTERS

Chapter 10 Leadership, Complicit Repercussions and False Security 107

Chapter 11 CouRage--When Action Is the Only Option 117

Chapter 12 Ubuntu--All Matters Matter 125

Chapter 13 Remembering Self 139

Preface

It was a Tuesday afternoon when I walked into a Black faculty reception and was graciously greeted by a friend, colleague, mentor and former Department Head of Africana Studies. His smile was infectious. We embraced, promised to have lunch soon and I departed. That was the last time I would embrace my friend. He died the next evening.

Stricken with grief, I laid in bed for days weeping. I was paralyzed with sorrow. As faith would have it, on the fourth day, a calendar invite message popped up on my phone reminding me of a previously scheduled lunch meeting with another colleague, the former and first African-American dean, who had been relieved from his duties 16 months after his arrival. Although I desperately wanted to cancel the meeting, I mustered up strength to meet him at a local eatery near campus. When I arrived, I started crying uncontrollably. I quickly ran to the bathroom, washed my face and tried to regain composure. I didn't fully understand what was happening; however, as we began to talk, the weight of my grief unlocked a sea of memories that illuminated the personal and professional destruction of countless Black and Brown faculty and staff at my institution. Flashes of emails, private conversations, open discussions and intimate knowledge of decisions to terminate or demote Black and

Brown colleagues—including my own personal "near-death" career experience—awakened my consciousness.

In that moment, I realized I was the carrier of these stories. I had witnessed the carnage firsthand. I was the overseer of the intellectual mill of death in my roles as the university's Associate Provost for Diversity and Inclusion, tenure-track faculty and athletic administrator. Impregnated with the seeds of half-truths about equality, meritocracy and the progress of diversity and inclusion, my soul began hemorrhaging the layers of destruction, pain and triumph; giving birth to a new, more elusive and refined truth.

Before I could tell the story of other Black and Brown professionals, the smell of death beckoned me to respond to my own personal destruction. I could no longer hide behind the professional shame of being marginalized, discarded and unjustly banished from my successful career in intercollegiate athletics. So, days after the funeral services for my friend, I dressed in my finest suit, went to the local IHOP and started writing.

Introduction

If Black women were free, it would mean that everyone else would have to be free since our freedom would necessitate the destruction of all the systems of oppression.

(Combahee River Collective Statement, 1977)

The following autoethnography takes an in-depth look into my 20-plus-year career that encompasses roles as an Associate Provost of Diversity and Inclusion, a tenure-track faculty member, a Director of Intercollegiate Athletics, a senior woman administrator and a former collegiate women's basketball coach and player.

An autoethnography is a form of self-reflection and writing that explores the subject's personal experience. It is a powerful tool to help inform, explain and examine complex social phenomenal through individual storytelling.

Storytelling can be traced back to ancient times. They are powerful tools that create meaning, connect communities and bring humans, inanimate objects and our subconscious thoughts to life. The use of storytelling narratives throughout this book is strategic and intentional. They are not simply used as a rhetorical strategy to convey my personal experiences, rather, an act of rebellion against the lack of discourse on how Black women navigate, define and thrive in higher education.

To be clear, the stories in this book are based on my interpretations of real-life experiences across various academic institutions, including a large urban research-intensive institution, a historically Black college and university and a small liberal arts Catholic university. They offer a bird's-eye view into the lessons I've learned and my unique set of personal and professional experiences inside and outside academe and intercollegiate athletics. They do not necessarily reflect the attitudes, practices and beliefs across all institutions for every Black woman. Institutions, racism and people are far too complex to be explained through any single set of experiences. However, I hope my narratives offer readers what I call the "experience of chance" that these kinds of behaviors, practices and systematic oppressive acts could and might happen in academia and other workplace environments.

The personal narratives in this book serve three primary functions. The first few chapters of the book—"Early ways of knowing" narratives—highlight, acknowledge and name my personal gifts and the guiding values and principles that anchor my perspective on leading and leadership. They highlight how my childhood experiences influenced my personal and professional style of leadership. They also embody a rite of passage through which I define, navigate and discover exactly how my individual beliefs and actions shaped the way I understand the world around me, organizations and leadership in general.

Second, the book is a direct critique of liberalism and the ideology of meritocracy as a solution to ending racism in higher education. The narratives unpack the effects of uninterrogated decision-making in higher education and intercollegiate athletics, revealing the hidden truth behind a false sense of security that protection is earned with long tenure, a clean HR record, outstanding evaluations, a respected reputation and hard-work ethic. It is also an outright assault on the academy's insidious love affair with the words diversity and inclusion, and the lack of dangerous discourse about institutional diversity and how it fails faculty, staff and students of color. To be clear, the lack of student, staff and faculty diversity in higher education and other organizations— and the perpetual failure of people of color—cannot simply be explained using the ideology of intellectual inferiority. Arguments like "he/she was not a good fit" or "it just didn't work out" ring hollow. In some cases, the failure lies in the racial and cultural ignorance of a heavily white administration and faculty. Rather than simply examining these particular justifications as a byproduct of happenstance, I propose that diversity leaders examine these excuses as longtime strategies that sustain the status quo even while they purport to upend it.

Throughout my career I've mentored hundreds of young Black women working two jobs, going to school full time and raising families, who believe that meritocracy offers a viable path to economic, political and social parity, only to earn 63 cents on the dollar compared to their White male and female counterparts. Their experiences, as well as my own, have shaped my belief that meritocracy can be both dangerous and disingenuous. Finally, the narratives demonstrate how even academic excellence and breaking racial and gender barriers fail to provide even modest safety or protection for Black women in the workplace.

In the closing chapters, I offer a new way of conceptualizing leadership and diversity and inclusion using an African philosophy called Ubuntu, which translates as: *"I am because you are, and you are because I am."* Ubuntu's humanist perspective highlights the interconnectedness of my personal story and the stories of others. It demonstrates that my story is not new. It's simply another way of telling the same unfortunate story to those who find single stories unbelievable. Through the use of Ubuntu, I hope to offer the reader a different perspective on leadership and leading. Because when we really get it right, we will discover a deeper understanding of our collective humanity and interconnection with one another—I am because you are, and you are because I am.

Together, these narratives recognize, celebrate and examine the struggles, leadership and the practical wisdom Black women have to offer higher education, intercollegiate athletics, and diversity and inclusion. I pray the stories in this book empower all women, especially women of color, who have questioned their intellectual, spiritual, political, cultural or leadership capacity. Know that you are not alone. Writing this book was a spiritual journey. A reminder that #BlackGirlMagic is more than a 21st century hashtag. It is about owning and embracing the magical journey that I and so many other Black women dare to imagine. Ultimately, it is a display of resilience, courage and the exploration of just how much extra shit Black women have to endure.

As David Goldberg[1] states: "Depending on how stories or experiences are understood, interpreted and framed, existence is recognized,

1 D.T. Goldberg, ed., *Anatomy of Racism* (Minneapolis, MN: University of Minnesota Press, 1990).

ignored and assigned significance; rendering the subject invisible within hierarchies." Under the backdrop and historical contexts of the Black Lives Matter movement, people of color, Black women especially, cannot afford invisibility.

So come along for the ride as I examine my own leadership, my own freedom and my own ability to transform the world. As the beginning quote suggests, my freedom is intricately linked to the freedom of others, for it necessitates the destruction of systems of oppression and the beginning of a new life.

Thought of the Day

Black Girl Magic in the Academy
Black girls rock.
We rock steady
And in rhythm to the
Whispered commands of God,
To the drums of our ancestors
To Jazz and Hip Hop
We are the essence of rhythm.
Our hips swaying to
The beat of our drums.
We rock to our own rhythm.
We are the vessels through which
Every generation is born.
We are the birth mothers of Truth
Of Micah, Sandra, Trayvon, Raynetta, Tamir, Kindra,
Michael, Joyce, Eric, Ralkina, Freddy and Alex.
The birth mothers of martyrs and revolutions
Because BLACK LIVES MATTER.
We have built underground railroads and media empires.
We were made in the image of God.
When I meet God,
Mahogany Queen of Queens
And see my image reflected,
I will smile.
For it is In
Her that
I have found myself.
Beautiful, Strong, Black and Proud.

I am She.
And She is Me.
I will shout Glory Hallelujah
As such profound joy reverberates throughout my soul
Making a joyful noise
Heard throughout space and time.
She with her Angela Davis 'fro asks if
I am my sister's keeper.
I will answer loud and proud.
I have kept my sister well.
We have to give honor
To the women who have gone before us,
Stand strong with the ones travelling with us,
And clear the way
For the ones coming after us.
Written by Evelyn Thompson
Copyright © April 2016

Journal Entry #1: Tell Your Story

1. Take a critical dive into what story(ies) must be told before you can move forward. What seeds of "truth or untruth" must you tell at this moment?

2. How is each story (or stories) connected to your personal and professional beliefs?

PART 1

Bird's-Eye View: Define and Navigate

1

Define: In Search of My Mother's Gardens

And when we go in search of our mothers' gardens,
it's not really to learn who trampled on them or
how or even why—we usually know that already.
Rather, it's to learn what our mothers planted
there, what they thought as they sowed and how
they survived the blighting of so many fruits.

—Sherley Anne Williams, from the Foreword to Zora Neale Hurston, "Their Eyes Were Watching God," 1978

Much of who we are is based upon a set of collective experiences that confirm or challenge our collective thoughts and actions. I am no different. I was raised on welfare by a single mother who always seemed destined for greatness, though she could never fully grasp it in our small town. A top student in school, my mother was admitted into college where she planned to study business. She also received several lucrative job offers after high school. However, a few weeks before the start of school, she recalls how my alcoholic grandfather beat and threatened my grandmother with a gun, leaving my mother and her younger siblings homeless. Angry, hurt and exhausted by her dysfunctional home life, my mother often recalls, with deep regret and sadness in her eyes, her decision not to attend college and stay with her younger siblings.

With both strength and courage, my mother would later go on to single-handedly raise four successful children. I share this brief story because before I was Dr. Martin, I was simply Robin from Lonsdale—the tall, bossy girl raised on public assistance who struggled with reading and loved playing sports with the boys. I tell this story because my mother's story is my story. I am the living, breathing manifestation of her dreams and desires. Her struggle and successes have given me the confidence to stand proud with or without academic degrees, a full bank account or the fantasy of the perfect family. Truth be told, we all are here to live and lead exceptional lives.

My journey begins with four distinct principles that reveal my core understanding of myself and of leadership. These guiding principles and lessons include identifying and naming my personal gifts—the art of questioning and eyes wide open; and my understanding for the need to self-advocate and fight for justice, or as I call it, Slapping Becky. Finally, I share insight into the single most important guiding principle I use when I'm called to speak out on critical issues—one that forces to me act for my community—better known as the Esther Principle. Together, these gifts, guiding values and principles have shifted my perspective from seeing leadership as an individual pursuit to seeing leadership as a function of community.

The Esther Principle: For Such a Time as This

My mother always stressed the importance of spirituality and church. She exposed me to different religious experiences, too—Christian, Unitarian, Presbyterian and nondenominational. Sunday school, prayer meetings, choir rehearsals and community revivals forged in me an unbreakable value system that over time has profoundly shaped and grounded my ideas about leadership and leading.

The biblical story of Esther, for example, serves as a powerful metaphor for my life and professional career. It's one of few stories in the Bible I remember vividly from my childhood, and one that I apply to my daily life. The story of Esther is about a beautiful Jewish woman who married the king of Persia, who did not know she was Jewish. Her uncle Mordecai warned her not to disclose her Jewish heritage, not even to the king, because of anti-Jewish sentiment in Persia.

Sometime later, the king was persuaded to issue a command to kill all of the country's Jews, including young people, old people, women and children. Mordecai overheard the plan and immediately went to Queen Esther to see if she would make an appeal to the king on behalf of the Jewish people. Esther was afraid. She knew that she could be killed for even making the petition, as well as for disclosing her Jewish heritage. Still, Mordecai pleaded his case, stating: "For if you remain silent at this time, relief and deliverance for the Jews will arise from another place, but you and your father's family will perish. And who knows, but that you have come to your royal position for such a time as this?" (Esther 4:14NIV).

My life has been filled with "Esther" moments, times when as a poor Black girl, I found myself thrust into "royal" positions and opportunities. I've been a first-generation college student, a first African-American female director of athletics, and the only African-American or woman in numerous leadership positions. My career path constantly reminds me of the enormous gift and burden of my "unseemly" heritage, so much so that Mordecai's phrase— "For who knows, but that you have come to this royal position for such a time as this"—has not only guided my actions, it has also transformed the way I view leadership.

Just like Queen Esther, when I'm sitting at the king's table (in my case, sitting as the only Black female in senior staff meetings), I have been paralyzed with fear, distress, anxiety and even doubt about whether I was deserving of my lofty positions. It is in these moments of doubt or questioning that I plead to my inner self and ask, *"What if I have come to this royal position for such a time as this?"* This singular principle has not only guided my actions but also, over time, transformed the way I view my individual privilege, power and responsibility, shifting my individualist perspective to a much grander idea of what it means to lead in community. It is what gives me confidence and the courage to act on behalf of myself and others.

We will all have Esther moments in our lives—times when it might be easier to close our eyes, wrestle with fear and wait. However, overtime, I've learned to acknowledge my fear in each situation, while not allowing it to consume and control all my actions. I've learned that every action, including silence, produces a reaction; and every reaction leads to a consequence. Consequences are inescapable.

As a result, I've become more intentional in opening my eyes, acknowledging both my fears and my abilities to meet the challenges at hand and ask that important question: "What if I have come to this royal position for such a time as this?"

Eyes Wide Open

I worshiped my brilliant, funny and charismatic brother, Robert, for his many talents, but one in particular stood out: his ability to sleep with his eyes open. Every Sunday as church services got underway, he would slowly drift off to sleep with his eyes wide open, evading both the sermon and the watchful eye of my mother. Years passed before one Sunday, as his slumber gave way to a snore, my mother realized he could sleep with his eyes open.

Over the years, I've come to see Robert's unnerving capacity reflected in my own struggle to accept my limited ability to ignore and tolerate pretense. Sometimes I wonder, as I watch injustice unfold and remain unaddressed: *Is it really possible to sleep with your eyes open?*

Unlike my brother, I never mastered the eyes-wide-open sleeping trick. In fact, I have the opposite reaction in difficult situations—my eyes are always open. Whether sitting in meetings, talking with colleagues and friends, or simply watching the news, oftentimes I vividly see the conflict, the dangerous question or the possible solution before others. Both my eyes and my spirit have an insatiable appetite for pondering what is being presented and what is hidden.

Despite this gift, throughout my career, I've entered meetings determined not to see, speak out or ask the difficult questions.

I've spent countless hours preparing and rehearsing dispassionate responses, developing strategies to avoid difficult discussions and using non-directive language. I've even practiced silence. Despite my efforts, I have never fully been able to circumvent my eyes-always-open gift, nor has this gift ever afforded me much rest.

I tell my brother's story because I've come to view my eyes-always-open reality as a gift. It helps me see my discomfort as a pathway to advocate for change. And while at times this gift feels like a 500–pound elephant sitting on my chest, pressuring me to return to safety and ease, it has also allowed to me see extraordinary transformations in people and organizations.

Embracing both my Esther moments and my eyes-wide-open reality has led me to an even deeper understanding. It has taught me that often the very traits or personal attributes that seem burdensome or unwanted, are in fact our greatest strengths and treasures. In "Seven Leadership Lessons for Minorities and Everyone Else," Umair Haque[2] sums up this reality beautifully:

> Those of [us] who are born different are the truly privileged ones. For it is our calling to live truly exceptional lives. While we may damn the weight of the burden, let us also give thanks for the gift.

---

2 Umair Haque, "Seven Leadership Lessons for Minorities and Everyone Else," Medium (blog), December 29, 2015, https://medium.com/bad-words/six-leadership-lessons-for-minorities-and-everyone-else-bc2278dc289b

The Art of Questioning

You know why the hard questions must be asked. It is not altruism, it is self-preservation—survival.

—Audre Lorde, Oberlin College Commencement Address, 1989

In my childhood neighborhood, the art of questioning was often dangerous and unwelcomed. Statements like, "Because I said so," "Who are you talking back to?" and "Sit down and shut up before I give you something to cry about," were the pervasive parenting strategies.

But my mother was different. She believed in the art of questions, sometimes ad nauseam. Whenever my siblings or I was suspected of misbehaving, we endured hourlong lectures—or as we called them "trials"—that required an opening statement of explanation, a logical defense for our behavior, and a counterargument for why she shouldn't spank us.

After years of practice, this gift of questioning has become second nature. At school, I became known as the curious kid in the back of the room who asked the difficult questions no one wanted to ask or answer. Like my mother, I began to enjoy the hunt for answers and the thrill of discovery. At times, my questioning skills were celebrated; other times, they were seen as dangerous. I quickly learned that a poorly placed question can prove hazardous to one's health.

For example, I once asked my mother why she made us pray every week that God bless us with $1 million, when we could just ask God to send us $100 trillion, and we wouldn't have to pray ever again. In my little-kid way I hungered to understand why God selected some families to suffer and provided others with abundance. But questioning God's power and decisions didn't go over well with my mother. I realized that when my siblings slowly backed out of the room, abandoning me to face the penalty of offending "Judge Gladys" alone.

This encounter would not be the first or the last time my love for inquiry and critical questioning left me feeling isolated and alone. At the peak of my professional career, I came to quickly identify friends and colleagues who also slowly backed out of the room or conversations to evade the path of conflict out of fear. This valuable lesson solidified my confidence, courage and ability to stand alone and firm in my resistance to authority. For I learned that deep inquiry, or the art of questioning, is not simply a function of getting the "right" answer; it is the conduit that sparks innovation that transforms people, places and entire organizations. The need to be right is a byproduct of ego and power. The need for deep inquiry is about social change.

No matter the outcome of my trials in the court of Gladys, those early life lessons cultivated my love for deep inquiry, my appreciation for diverse discourse and my thirst for social justice. They have guided my path toward self-awareness, allowed me to deeply connect with those around me and given me a greater understanding of the interdependence of the world around me.

Slapping Becky

By age 11, I was a masterful diplomat and activist. I could articulate what I wanted, defend my position and offer win/win solutions. That was right around the time I entered middle school and discovered the unfortunate perils of privilege.

Becky was her name—a wealthy white girl who regularly bullied other students with impunity. Unfortunately for Becky, though I was taught never to pick a fight. I was also taught never to run from a bully. So when Becky called me "darkie" and spat on my leg in class, I calmly rose from my desk and slapped her across the face. Shock echoed across the room.

I spent the next two hours in the principal's office until my mother picked me up. I felt both embarrassed and liberated. I knew it was wrong to fight in school, and I was not proud of that moment. However, I stood my ground when the principal suggested I be suspended from school and Becky be moved to another class because she felt threatened.

With my mother by my side, I refused to accept the lopsided punishment, especially given my stellar record of compliance and Becky's history of lawless actions. I asked the principal to justify his initial decision, and questioned whether Becky's race and socioeconomic status helped shape his decision to dispense unequal punishment. As my mother tells the story, I "sassed" the principal until Becky and I received the same punishment. We both served two-day suspensions, and Becky stayed clear of my path for the remainder of the school year.

The Becky incident taught me that violence is never the solution to a conflict; however, neither is apathy. I learned that while self-advocacy will not eradicate all injustice, it is, where the fight for justice begins.

Collectively, these "early ways of knowing" helped me understand my individual role and responsibility in this world. They taught me that while it seems easier to close my eyes, wrestle with fear and wait for another time or opportunity, there is an Esther moment in all of us. For we all have come to such a time as this to create change for our communities, families and organizations.

For me, that meant I had to learn how to lead in strange places, always keep my eyes open, ask questions and fight for social justice. These "early ways of knowing" taught me that effective leaders rarely possess the ability to sleep with their eyes fully closed.

Thought of the Day

In order to see the world and others around us, we must first acknowledge and own our individual existence. We must identify, name and claim our unique gifts and attributes no matter how difficult, weird or insufficient we believe those gifts to be. For our gifts or 'early ways of knowing' guide our path to self-discovery, give us wisdom, and more importantly, grant us permission to be exactly who we are.

Journal Entry #2: Remembrance of Self

1. Share 1-3 stories that describe or explain who you are. List the personal traits, attributes and gifts that make you unique (e.g. slapping Becky, eyes-wide-open, art of questioning). Note that these aren't necessarily the traits others compliment you about, though they might be.

2

NAVIGATE: FILL THE ROOM AND KNOW YOUR NAME

For while the tale of how we suffer, and how we are delighted, and how we may triumph is never new, it always must be heard. There isn't any other tale to tell, it's the only light we've got in all this darkness.

—James Baldwin, "Sonny's Blues," 1957

The following narratives explore key early career lessons that further shaped, affirmed and challenged my perspectives. Through them, I uncovered lessons about overcoming fear, "knowing my place" as a Black female and the dangerous seduction of valuing Black exceptionalism over collectivism.

The narratives harken back to my fascination with difficult questions, my dedication to finding answers and my inability to blindly accept injustice. They uncover my profound journey of self-awareness and purpose.

Finally, these early career experiences helped strengthened my confidence, understand the power and impact of my gifts and voice, and allowed me to truly embrace the Esther principle.

Fear of Being Great

My entrance into higher education was neither conscious nor intentional. My 6-foot-3-inch frame and my exceptional ability to run fast and jump high landed me a full athletic scholarship to play women's basketball at the University of New Orleans. It was the first time I had left my impoverished neighborhood for any extended length of time and the first time I began to imagine a life of unlimited possibilities.

I remember everything about college. My first day of class, my first walk on Bourbon Street, my first basketball practice, the dreaded preseason workouts and Sybil Blalock, the 5-foot-6-inch assistant coach. She challenged everything I thought I knew about hard work, sacrifice, teamwork, fear and success.

Every day during my first preseason workouts, I woke up with a headache, a nauseous stomach and bouts of anxiety. I feared the harsh workouts, the extra running, the heavy weights and the painful cramps. Despite my natural talents, I had never worked that hard in my life; I was crippled with fear. I thought Coach Blalock would literally cause me to drop dead of a massive heart attack. After just two weeks of preseason work, I called my mother and begged her to take me out of school. I was ready to quit; I was fearful I didn't have the strength to continue.

Ten minutes into what she called my complaining session, I noticed an eerie silence on the other end of the call. My mother had hung up. She was over my excuses. While I dreaded the harsh workouts and Coach Blalock, my mother sensed a greater fear—of me returning home and giving up an opportunity to attend college. So, instead of listening or cosigning onto my mess, she did the best thing she could do for her child: She made me face my greatest fear—the fear of being GREAT.

Somewhere deep inside, the fear of being pushed beyond my comfort and the familiar paralyzed me. To be sure, this was a new experience.

Growing up poor, I knew a little something about competition. As the tomboy in the group, I was comfortable tackling the boys, playing football and fighting in the streets. Competition had always been easy; I was a good athlete. However, Coach Blalock demanded something different, something more. Competition had an opponent, an adversary. But she asked me to compete against myself. She asked me to run my personal best and then expected an even better result the next day. Her expectations scared the hell out of me.

After my mother hung up on me, I returned to practice. Where else would I go? I worked harder for Coach Blalock and for myself, and I never looked back. I learned that fear is the enemy of all success. The real battle is not against opponents or adversaries; it's against ourselves. Once I had conquered the internal demons telling me, "You are not smart enough, you are not fast enough, you're from the wrong neighborhood, this is too hard," I knew I'd won the game.

Similarly, the game of life is, to a large degree, an internal battle that requires personal truth, courage and endurance. Nelson Mandela once said, "Courage is not the absence of fear, but triumph over it. The brave man is not he who does not feel afraid, but he who conquers that fear."

Being a Division I student-athlete pushed me beyond my limited imagination of greatness. I was fortunate to play alongside other strong women. As I pushed myself, I watched them, and I learned how to become successful. These lessons of strength, perseverance and teamwork solidified my approach to life's challenges. They gave me the self-confidence to know, to really know, that I could handle any situation. This early lesson stayed with me throughout my career.

Know Your Place: Listen, Don't Speak

When you know your name, you should hang on to it, for unless it is noted down and remembered, it will die when you do.

—Toni Morrison, "Song of Solomon," 1977

After a successful college basketball career and graduation, I accepted a graduate assistant coaching position for the women's basketball team at my alma mater. This was my first job out of college, and after being surrounded by great teammates and the leadership of Coach Blalock, I was full of confidence and strength. I was ready to rid the world of its problems—that is, until I was asked to "listen and not be heard." It was one the earliest memories that shaped my professional career and my understanding of the difficult terrain of being Black and female in the workplace.

Like any good graduate assistant, I was eager. I worked hard and focused on doing everything the right way. I was the first one in the office every day and the last one to leave. Within a few months of my arrival, the head coach organized a staff retreat to plan for the upcoming season. Weeks before the retreat, I started preparing my notes and drawing up offensive and defensive strategies I thought would help the team. The retreat began, and the coach asked everyone for their input.

I was prepared. I patiently waited my turn to speak and then offered my feedback. I was excited to share my ideas and provided detailed justifications for my recommendations.

Impressed by my thoughtful input, the head coach decided to incorporate several of my ideas and thanked the entire staff for their hard work and insight. I left the meeting feeling great. More importantly, I thought the team had come up with some great ideas to improve the program. I was excited about the future.

The next day, one of the more experienced assistant female coaches walked into my office, shut the door and said these dreaded words: *"We need to talk."*

She started the conversation by saying how much she valued my energy and ability to work with student-athletes while maintaining a high level of discipline. She expressed how happy she was that I was on the team.

However, she added, she had one minor concern. "You overstepped your boundary in the retreat," she said. Confused, I instinctively engaged my skills in the art of questioning. I asked for clarification.

I requested that she give me an explicit example of when I had "overstepped my boundary." She offered no specific example or clear answer. So, I probed further.

"Do you believe my ideas and recommendations would help the team?" I asked.

"Oh, yes, I do, and I support implementing your strategies and ideas," she said. She then proceeded to express her grave concerns regarding my level of assuredness given my "limited experience and role" on the staff.

That led to my final question: *"Are you upset about the ideas for improvement, or that the ideas came from me?"*

Stunned by my question and my apparent audacity to confront the situation directly, she abruptly ended the meeting with string of unfounded and emotionally charged statements:

"I just feel like. I didn't like it when you said . . ."

"I think you could have said it another way."

Over the years, I've heard these phrases and variations on them used to communicate a much more subtle and sinister underlying message: "Stay in your place. You are best seen and not heard." This kind of behavior always reminds me of the scene in Lee Daniels' movie "The Butler" when Annabeth tells Cecil Gaines, played by Forest Whitaker, "When you're serving, I don't even want to hear you breathe. The room should feel empty when you're in it."

My entire career is full of stories of people trying to put me in my place or asking me to pretend the room is empty when I'm it.

Fortunately for me, I never learned that lesson. Being silent and complicit contradicts every value that Gladys Martin ever taught me. I never learned how to be invisible or how to sleep with my eyes closed. And since my *eyes are always open*, so is my mouth.

As a Black woman, I've come to believe that knowing my place and staying in my place are two different things. Knowing my place is about understanding the social, political and individual contributions I bring to my position of power. Staying in my place, though, is an act of oppression, whether self-imposed or externally enforced. It is designed to ensure current power structures remain intact. Staying in one's place is an act of personal, spiritual and mental sabotage.

The Next Good Job

Eventually, I left the college program and accepted a full-time position at a private independent high school. I was the first full-time, African-American female coach at the school. I was 25 years old, had great colleagues, a supportive staff and a good basketball team. It was an exciting time in my life.

After 16 months on the job and a successful season, a few helicopter parents began to express typical parental concerns like: Who would be the starting point guard next year? How much playing time on the court would their child have? They complained about the grueling practice schedule and workouts. Some parents even got involved in off-campus student conflicts.

Because this was my first high-school coaching position, I spent a lot of time reassuring parents and administrators that every student-athlete would be treated fairly and that everyone would have an opportunity to participate on the team. That summer, the athletic director (AD) and I spent a lot of time together working through various parent issues.

Because of our close relationship, I knew something was terribly wrong the moment the AD walked into my office at the beginning of the season. He explained that several parents had voiced anxieties over my decision to play at an all-Black public school located in a "dangerous" neighborhood. They cited concerns about possible violence and fear of the impact of playing in a hostile environment. Because of the concerns, he recommended we either increase security, hire a police escort for the team or cancel the game.

I was perplexed. The two teams had played against each other in previous years without any problems. There was a positive history between the two teams and no obvious reason for the new measures. So I began probing. I asked whether race, class and privilege were fueling the parents' unease. After asking this question, I quickly recognized this exchange as another "Slapping Becky" moment.

Frustrated by my questions and my questioning, the AD offered me a choice: either accept the extra security and police escort or cancel the game. His demeanor and language felt like another order to stay in my place. And while he later apologized for his stern temperament, he reaffirmed his decision and security concerns, citing that it was his duty to protect the staff, student-athletes, and parents. He added that race, class and privilege had nothing to do with his decision. He concluded the meeting by expressing his sincere disappointment in my line of questioning regarding racism and classism and reminded me of the progress and advances the school had made toward diversity with my appointment.

Days later, I reluctantly agreed to the extra police security, but not before I offered my own request for extra security when the team played an all-White school who openly brandished the Confederate flag and frequently hurled racist comments from the stands. As the only personal of color on the staff, I expressed my fears and deep concern for my safety and reminded him of his responsibility to protect student-athletes, parents, and in this case me, the staff person.

Then I officered a closing statement: *"You can't call them a nigger and not call me one, too. I am not the exception; I am the students at the higher school. When you see them, I hope you see me."* Shocked registered on his face, and he quickly ended the conversation.

This was my first full-time job. I was the only African-American in the department. I knew my unwavering stance in this particular situation could result in termination or at least, create an adverse rapport with my new boss, players' parents, and other community leaders. I knew what was at stake; yet I also knew that I couldn't remain silent. In this case, I chose not to yield to racism and classism. I had to fight against the seduction of Black exceptionalism by aligning myself with the kids in the "bad" neighborhood. Otherwise, my tenure at this school could have be detrimental both to my personal conscience and my professional livelihood. I was more afraid of losing myself than preserving the status quo. This was a pivotal moment in my career—an Esther moment when I chose to stand up instead of acquiescing.

A few days later, the AD came back to my office and decided against having a police escort at the game with the all-Black school. Both teams played well and without confrontation. We simply moved past the incident.

From this experience, I learned that every action produces a reaction, and every reaction has a consequence. When people ask me about being courageous or taking an opposing stance on a topic, I'm reminded that consequences are inescapable—silence is, in itself, a choice. I also learned the dangers of believing in exceptionalism—that intellect, work ethic and integrity alone determine one's fate. In fact, I came to suppose that the belief in exceptionalism is the root of prejudice, fear, discrimination and exclusion. It not only gives a false illusion of equal starting lines, but also masks a dark lie.

Growing up, I watched smart, honest and hardworking people engulfed and devastated by life challenges and unforeseen circumstances every day. They lost jobs and homes, went hungry and lacked access to the best teachers and healthcare. I quickly learned that intellect, work ethic and integrity didn't guarantee success for my neighbors. These early lessons helped me abandon the idea that I was smarter, more deserving or even more righteous than anyone else. In short, they taught me humility and my individual role and responsibility as a leader.

I conclude this chapter with a "Thought of the Day" and a reminder that others cannot, and will not define or determine my destiny.

Thought of the Day

Do you know how many people have tried to shut me up? You are certainly not the first and won't be the last. I carry with me the wisdom of truth, the prosperity of knowledge and the spirit of God. I have neither a designated place nor length of time for which I can stay. I determine my place and remain strong in the gifts, skills and talents I carry forth in service of the collective humanity.

So starting today, I will no longer question or allow others to question the complex path that lies before me. It is a path built on the backs of my ancestors and a path to which I must fully commit. My place is destined for greatness. It is preordained, derived from a place of strength and hard work. I owe nothing in particular, yet I am indebted to those who have come before, those I currently serve and those who will tend to my remains. So, I journey on, no longer bound by the illusion of place but rather by the discovery of how my individual gifts, talents and resources can produce and nurture new life for individuals and organizations.

Journal Entry #3: Finding Your Place

1. Share a time when someone tried to "put you in your place." How did you handle the situation? How would you handle the situation today?

2. Complete the following statement: My place is …

3

DISCOVER: IN THE STORM

Where justice is denied, where poverty is enforced, where ignorance prevails and where any one class is made to feel that society is in an organized conspiracy to oppress, rob and degrade them, neither persons nor property will be safe.

—Frederick Douglass, speech on the 24th anniversary of emancipation, Washington, D.C., 1886

In 2004, I returned to New Orleans and accepted a position at Dillard University as the first African-American female director of athletics (AD) and head women's basketball coach. I was appointed by the interim female president for whom I had worked previously. She was strong, smart and demanding. I was excited for the challenge.

My first few months as the AD were tenuous; I had replaced the former AD, who had been reassigned as the men's basketball coach. Only two weeks separated the time in which he moved out of the office and I moved in. It was an awkward arrangement to say the least.

During my first few months on the job, I worked hard to repair the relationship and affirm my support for the former AD; however, I was clear that I was in charge. It was my first AD job, the department had made significant progress during my short tenure, and I made it a point to tell everyone about all the wonderful changes I had made. I was great, particularly in my own mind.

One day in a staff meeting, I began to highlight the enormous improvements I had made in the department since my arrival. I noted such accomplishments as increased fundraising and marketing, improved facilities, reduced department spending and increased effectiveness. From the outside, everything looked like it was moving in the right direction, until one of the staffers openly complained about some of the changes.

The meeting became heated. And I put the entire staff on trial. I was Gladys, the judge, jury and prosecutor; and more importantly, I was right. I shut down any conversation that opposed or threatened the changes that had been made. I let the staff know that under no circumstance would I allow anyone to thwart what I perceived as drastic improvements. I left the meeting beaming with gratification and delight that I was in charge.

Later that evening driving through my neighborhood, I glanced at a yard sign at a local church. The sign read, *"What if you are wrong?"* I almost wrecked my car. Was that sign for me? Was this some practical joke? Had I become the bully Becky in the Slapping Becky narrative?

Before that moment, I had never considered the consequences of my condescending actions and dismissive behavior. I had never considered that I could be wrong. I had never imagined that even though I made the right decisions, the process and the interrogation of the staff was the wrong approach.

This entire experience taught me that I had never been in control. The opposite was true. I had misused my position of power and the art of questioning to demean the staff. I had lost sight of what was really important—teamwork and leadership. The episode caused me to reflect on and then shift away from this autocratic leadership style. I saw the sign at the church as a divine intervention and spent the remaining time in this position listening more and talking less.

Hurricane Katrina

After I spent months learning valuable lessons on how to become a better leader, the city of New Orleans and the Gulf Coast region were devastated by Hurricane Katrina.

Early on a Saturday morning, I attended the funeral of a prominent community leader. The funeral lasted several hours, and like many people at the ceremony, I was unaware of the enormous danger heading to New Orleans and the Gulf Coast.

Even though there were no clouds in the sky, my phone began to ring, as players, coaches and administrative staff requested details about an evacuation plan. Evacuation plans? I quickly left the funeral, received an update and sprang into action. The next several hours remain a blur. I organized the teams and staff, locked down the facilities and ensured everyone had an evacuation plan. Later that evening,

I packed a three-day supply of clothes and toiletries and headed to Houston, Texas. I was confident I would return to the comforts of my life in a few days.

Days later, I watched as images of devastation and death flashed across our TV screens: broken levees; people on rooftops pleading for their lives; images of the elderly, the disabled and thousands of people living in poverty slowly dying in the heat. It broke both my heart and spirit.

There I was, watching the tragedy of my home city unfold from the comfort of a nice hotel room in Houston — a state away from the stark realities of my neighbors. I was one of the lucky ones. I could afford gas, the travel expenses and an inflated hotel rate. I had friends and an entire community in Houston — people who reached out and ensured that I was well taken care of.

Days, then weeks, then months passed before I returned to the city of New Orleans. But I never returned to my apartment, which had suffered major flood damage. Like so many others, the storm impacted every aspect of my life.

I had limited access to bank accounts and financial records, my cell phone service, clothing and daily necessities. I remember — like it was yesterday — the surrealness of being a high-ranking leader in higher education who had to stand in line for hours to sign up for public assistance, apply for my Federal Emergency Management Agency (FEMA) number and purchase clothes at the local Walmart.

I remember how the weight of the experience began to take its toll, and I remember the moment when I no longer could mask my devastation.

It was about six weeks after the storm when I walked into the nearest Red Cross to request housing assistance. And that's when I suddenly began to cry. The Red Cross volunteer recognized my trauma; she took a little extra time to help me find temporary housing at a local extended-stay hotel. I will never forget the moment I walked into that hotel; it was the first time in months I felt any semblance of normal.

My eyes-wide-open trait was on full display. My experiences during Hurricane Katrina forced me to fully grasp my financial, mental and spiritual vulnerability. Yes, I had grown up in poverty. But Hurricane Katrina and its aftermath marked the first time that, as a college graduate, I reflected upon my personal journey from poverty to "middleincomeness," and along with it, the ideology of meritocracy. Because despite all my hard work, my good-paying job and my education, I wasn't any different than the thousands of other storm victims. The FEMA lines were not separated by the haves and the have-nots. There was only one line, and we all had to take our turn. For many of us, especially for me, Hurricane Katrina served as a great equalizer. It exposed and dismantled my belief that I was assured protection from poverty because of my education and status in life. This ideology of meritocracy flew in the face of my new reality and reminded me of my interdependence upon others.

Hurricane Katrina brought home basic lessons of humanity as well as recognition of the fragile tapestry upon which our collective democracy, freedoms and financial stability rest. It taught me the power of giving, receiving and unconditional caring as I watched people across this country reach across communities to help strangers. It also gave me firsthand experiences in managing a crisis, and of course, illustrated the impact of effective and ineffective leadership.

The enormity of the storm challenged our political system, social morals and individual capacities to lead. I watched leaders ignore and fail thousands of citizens for days. I watched leaders once regarded as pillars of the community commit fraud, lie and betray the public to serve their own interests. I watched organizations, including my university, struggle to develop, organize and articulate a strategy and vision for recovery.

The storm also showed me more. It reminded me that leadership demands attention to the work and the worker, to humans and humanity, to skills and talents. It also taught me that while leaders lead in times of conflict, managers start and exacerbate that conflict. I watched organizations with great leaders quickly devise, communicate and implement strategies that enabled their organizations not only to survive Hurricane Katrina but also to flourish in its aftermath. On the contrary, organizations led by people who relied on positional power created panic and instability throughout the community.

The latter statement is not meant to place judgment, rather to acknowledge that leadership and leading are difficult under normal conditions; a disaster like Hurricane Katrina magnifies both the enormous difficulty and impact leadership has on organizations, people and communities.

The entire experience of Hurricane Katrina changed the way I viewed my individual responsibility as a leader and leadership in general. As a result, 10 years after Hurricane Katrina, I enrolled in a doctoral program to learn more about leadership, leaders and organizational change management. I became particularly interested in leadership within the Black community.

So when asked in my doctoral application, "What is the importance of effective leadership?" I reflected upon my Hurricane Katina experience and wrote:

> *When effective leadership is present in the urban community, it centers around personal and global accountability and responsibility, truth, nonjudgmental respect, open dialogue, in-depth personal and communal relationships, and a collective sense that the stability and success of the urban community depends on collective individuals. It will evolve when the middle-class minorities reach out, engage, patronize and develop effective tools to support the marginalized. It will demand that urban community leaders revert from greed, gluttony and wasteful self-indulgence, all of which erode the sense of personal responsibility for the "least of them." Twenty-first century leadership will emulate the posture of service, inclusiveness, democratic civility, tolerance and respect, along with a high level of cultural competence. It will celebrate heritage and history and speak out against notions of intellectual inferiority and genocide. Effective leadership will demand that leaders constantly evolve. Lastly, it will be a global leadership approach that encompasses technology, human resources and social capital at its highest level. It will be a leadership model that will espouse the belief that we are our brothers' keepers.*

In "Dreams From My Father," Barack Obama writes candidly about the Rev. Jeremiah Wright, the pastor of Trinity United Church of Christ in Chicago. The Rev. Wright was the controversial minister who, during the 2008 election, was accused of espousing racial hate and division within his church. According to the book, the Trinity United Church of Christ created a set of guiding principles called the "Black Value System." Within that value system, the Rev. Wright wrote passionately about the principle of "A Disavowal of the Pursuit of Middleclassness":

While it is permissible to chase "middleincomeness" with all our might, those blessed with the talent or good fortune to achieve success in the American mainstream must avoid the psychological entrapment of Black "middleclassness" that hypnotizes the successful brother or sister into believing they are better than the rest and teaches them to think in terms of "we" and "they" instead of "US." (p. 284).

As a young Black professional in the midst of chasing "middleincomeness," I understood the unconscious mental entrapment that the Rev. Wright wrote about. Like so many first-generation middle-class African-Americans escaping the "hood," getting off welfare and buying a new car represented the American dream to me. Instead of going back into my community, I — like so many others — sought satisfaction in escaping it.

As I reflected upon my personal journey from poverty to "middleincomeness," I started becoming more and more aware of the need for leaders like myself to step up. I am a firm believer that the survival and stability of the urban communities lie not in the hands of big government, but in the efforts of each of us to forge viable commercial and economic partnerships and find sustainable and creative solutions to close the educational, economic and political gaps that plague our communities. As leaders, we must be tech-savvy, bilingual, multicultural, emotionally intelligent, transparent, globally focused, inclusive and multidimensional. We must continue to demand active, strategic leadership both from ourselves and others. For the change we seek, is within us—all of us.

Journal Entry #4: Effective Leadership

1. Define or describe the characteristics of an effective leader.

2. Describe a specific time or situation when you've exhibited the outlined characteristics. What were you responding to? What was the impact on the situation and relationships involved?

3. Describe a specific time when you struggled or failed to exhibit those effective leadership qualities and principles.

4. In what areas of leadership can you improve?

PART 2

EQUITY: RACE, GENDER AND ATHLETICS

4

Race: The 1 Percent Club

Caring for myself is not self-indulgence, it is self-preservation, and that is an act of political warfare.

—Audre Lorde, "A Burst of Light," 1988

A 2015 article in Forbes, "Why Aren't More Women Reaching the Top of College Sports," highlighted the disparate opportunities for women in intercollegiate athletics, pointing out that athletics is still very much a male-dominated industry. The article stated that of the 345 universities that sponsor sports on the NCAA Division I level, only 26 females—a mere 7.5 percent—were athletic directors, and only 1 percent were women of color.

As a former member of the 1 percent club (a Black female Athletics Director), I experienced firsthand the intersection of race and gender in athletics. The following narratives reveal the elusive nature of social, political and positional power for women in intercollegiate sports, especially women of color. They examine my roles as the first Black female athletic director at two NAIA schools and a senior associate director of athletics and senior woman administrator (SWA).

Elusive Positional Power

One year after Hurricane Katrina, the devastating effects of the storm still reverberated throughout New Orleans. Budget constraints forced my university to eliminate all the positions in athletics, and I was left to manage and lead the department. I worked day and night to remain positive and rebuild the program and the university. I used every ounce of social, political and professional capital I had to advance the department. My efforts were highlighted by the National Association of Collegiate Directors of Athletics when I received the Hurricane Katrina Leadership award.

Despite my efforts, I yearned for a simpler life. Instinctively I knew it was time to leave New Orleans. Limited housing options, mounds of debris on every street corner, the stench of death lurking around every corner and the fading memories of the life I once knew started to take a toll. Eight months after the storm, I applied and accepted a position as the first African- American female athletics director at a small Catholic university in Oakland, California.

During the interview process, my intuition screamed danger. I could sense this was not a great opportunity; however, I needed to leave New Orleans, and this was the best opportunity on the table. But there were warning signs. I was the only African-American administrator in the entire university. I was the only female in the athletics department. And to make matters worse, I learned that I had been selected to serve as AD over the men's basketball coach, who had been at the school for more than a decade.

The first week on the job, I sensed that the males on the staff preferred him to me. But the job was mine, so I started building relationships in the community, restructuring the department to maximize revenues, hiring a few coaches, developing a new website and marketing strategy and launching a new softball program. Our teams were highly successful, and the university president and other colleagues noticed the positive changes.

Despite my success, I never felt fully supported. Every one of my new initiatives was questioned or delayed. I got the sense that some of the males in the department not only resented the changes, they also resented the ensuing successes. I worked especially hard to include everyone in the decision-making process to avoid making the same leadership mishaps that plagued my previous position. This time, I focused on being more inclusive; however, I quickly realized that I was an outsider looking in, and this was an all-boys club—no women allowed.

One evening as I was heading home from work, I noticed a group of students and non-students in the gym after closing hours. As the AD, I asked the students to leave the gym so I could lock down the building. Angered by my request, one of the male student-athletes not only ignored me, he suggested others do the same. He argued that he was a student and had the right to use the gym at any time.

Shocked by his response, I became more forceful in my approach. I clearly informed the group of the gym's hours of operation and requested they leave the premises. The students eventually departed, but not before the male student-athlete walked dangerously close to me, aggressively asserting his disgust with me and the rules. Visibly shaken by the entire incident, I immediately locked up the facility, went home, had a glass of wine, sent a letter of reprimand to the coach to be sent to the student regarding his aggressive behavior and departed for a conference the following morning.

Still sickened by entire incident, I left several voice messages for my immediate supervisor the next day, desperately seeking support. After repeated calls, he returned my call to discuss the matter and inquire about the letter of reprimand. As I began to describe the incident, I was abruptly interrupted. He didn't seem concerned about my side of the story or about gathering details about how a student-athlete had physically threatened me. Instead, the hourlong conversation was spent scolding me and telling me how to handle the situation better in the future. He also questioned my authority to reprimand a student-athlete.

As the AD, I was totally blindsided by his response. I spent days replaying the episode in my mind. Nothing in my entire career had prepared me for this. I was the least respected, the least heard and, more importantly, the least protected in the university. It was my first real encounter with blatant disrespect, disregard and total humiliation in the workplace. The entire incident shook me to my core. I didn't know where to turn.

When I returned to my office, my direct supervisor scheduled a follow-up meeting. He reaffirmed his decision not to reprimand the student. I got the sense he wanted to see my expression when he delivered this news. I sat quietly and stared directly into his eyes, not wanting to give him the satisfaction of witnessing the rage I felt inside. As our meeting ended, I felt a single tear rush down my cheek.

In some strange way, I felt powerless and powerful in the same moment. Powerless in the way a Black woman's positional power is constantly being thwarted, undermined—elusive at times. Yet powerful because I decided to choose a different path. Unlike so many, I had the power, the opportunity and the confidence to simply move on. This painful incident taught me about the elusive nature of positional power as a Black woman.

After the meeting, I started to reflect upon my time at the university, the encounter with the student- athlete, my unsupportive direct supervisor and the somewhat hostile environment within the department. I walked back to my office, called several colleagues and started applying for other jobs. I never openly talked about the incident. I mostly stayed in my office for the remainder of my time at the university. And while some people suspected something was wrong, I pretended like nothing had happened. I realized that in my haste to leave the harsh conditions post-Hurricane Katrina, I had inadvertently run into a very different kind of storm.

Two months later, I was recruited and accepted a much more prestigious position, making more money at a bigger university. I never met with my direct supervisor to tell him I was leaving. I didn't want to give him the satisfaction. Instead, after I returned my signed contract, I scheduled a meeting with the president, thanked her for her support and the opportunity to serve and never looked back.

I rationalized the entire incident as a lesson in doing my due diligence and research before accepting a new position. I should have asked more questions about workplace culture, personnel and climate. I learned to never take a job without doing a 360-degree assessment of the organization, company or institution. I learned the importance of asking tough questions during interviews, researching former employees' tenures (especially the tenure of people of color and women) and calling other people in the industry to gain different insights.

In addition, I learned to try to connect with the person in the room who seems a little disengaged or disgruntled. I now ask questions directly to the committee members who are eerily silent, give nonverbal cues or who immediately leave the rooms after the interviews. While I am not suggesting that the opinion of a disgruntled employee should negate the positive attributes of an organization or that an unhappy worker will provide accurate information, I have found that these individuals are worth a closer, intentional look.

Finally, this experience also taught me to listen to my intuition and to pay careful attention to what is not being said. After years working in intercollegiate athletics and managing high-profile coaches, I've learned to invest very little into what is being said. This may sound contradictory, since we are taught to listen to understand before being understood. But as an African-American woman, I believe it is just as, if not more, important to listen for what my coworkers and colleagues don't say.

Here are two quick examples. Throughout the entire encounter with the aggressive student-athlete, my supervisor repeatedly stated his support for me. He even sent an email correspondence reaffirming his support and wishing me success. However, his failure to reprimand the student-athlete for his behavior and his suggestion that I review the department's hours of operation policy to avoid future negative encounters communicated a very different message.

When my peer assistant coach requested a separate meeting after our staff retreat to discuss and praise the recommendations I had offered to improve the department, she said she appreciated my insights, while also making it clear that I needed to stay in my place. Sometimes these kinds of nuances are overlooked because we want to give people the benefit of the doubt. We regularly view microaggressions as isolated incidents, perpetrated by a few mean-spirited people with good intentions, when in fact, many are intentional and calculated. Whether they are hidden in backroom conversations, innuendos or off-the-cuff remarks, these moments of blatant disrespect are rarely publicly addressed. Like clouds after a morning dew, they simply linger in the atmosphere, clouding everyone's vision and never illuminating the truth.

To be clear, I am not suggesting all Black women, people or organizations share homogeneous experiences, communication styles or policies. My goal here is not to make blanket statements or suggest that all universities or organizations are riddled with unconscious or conscious gender or racial biases. However, I am suggesting that minorities use best-practice interviewing techniques to identify organizations in which they are most likely to be able to contribute, thrive and enjoy a long tenure. Of course, these steps don't guarantee a lengthy and affirmative tenure with any organization. However, I've found that these practices give employees a broader context and awareness about the people, the environment and more importantly, the resources and threats that can aid or sabotage individual successes.

This awareness remains particularly important because, let's face it, people of color don't just lose jobs—we lose careers. So I close this chapter with the following "Thought of the Day."

Thought of the Day

Starting from the first day of work, you only have a certain amount of time to influence the change process. Think about it. You can probably only get people's buy-in for three new big ideas and maybe 20 small initiatives before they grow weary of your "know-it-all," "goodie-two-shoes," "I-know-better-than-you" attitude. Once people start to figure out that you changed their paradigm and the newness of your presence wears off, you can quickly find yourself at odds with everyone in the organization. People start to have conversations about your effectiveness, qualifications or, better yet, whether you are the "right fit" for the team. Marginalized and fearful of losing the very thing you worked so hard for, you find yourself in a precarious state: Do I stay in a place knowing that I have no, or limited, power and influence, or do I reinvent myself and look for another job? For many African-Americans, that is the real and difficult choice: Stay and start the degrading tango of the marginalized, or saddle up for the two-step of the wild, wild West and its likely blazing demise?

Thinking about the possibilities doesn't leave many options, but neither does denying the existence of the two choices. The purpose of knowing the two choices is not to breed fear but to empower you. In knowing, you hold all the cards because you understand your place, and you don't fear or resent the process. It is in this moment of awareness that you can understand your individual privilege, power and responsibility.

Journal Entry #5: Elusive Power

1. Describe a specific time when your positional power seemed elusive. Who was involved? What was at stake? How did you respond?

2. How did the incident change you? What was your biggest take away?

3. What, if anything, would you change about your response? Why?

5

GENDER: INTERNAL/ EXTERNAL CONSEQUENCES

Believe me, the reward is not so great without the struggle.

—Wilma Rudolph

One of the most difficult positions in intercollegiate athletics is the senior woman administrator's (SWA) position. Whether hiring more female coaches, addressing sexual harassment and pay inequalities, or fighting daily macro/microaggressions, the role of the SWA is often viewed in opposition to male coaches, administrators and budget directors. Even younger female staffers aren't automatic allies—some would rather be liked than principled; others are angling to replace you someday.

As the position title suggests, the SWA is the highest-ranking female on the executive team in the athletics department. The position was created, thanks to the Title IX movement, to ensure women had a voice at the table, access to resources, decision-making power and, importantly, to ensure universities adhered to Title IX legislation:

> *"Women shall not be excluded from participation in, be denied the benefits of or be subject to discrimination under any educational program or activity receiving federal financial assistance."*

As the associate athletics director and SWA, I was the executive administrator, with direct budget and operational oversight for 10 varsity programs, 24 coaches, 33 direct reports and the offices of Student-athlete Academic Support Services, Compliance and Rules Education, and Champs/Life Skills program. I also developed and administered a $1.8 million Title IX and Gender Equity Plan.

Just like in previous jobs, I jumped right in. My experiences at previous institutions prepared me to take on this new and complex set of responsibilities by transforming my leadership style and approach. I was more prepared to take on this role than I had ever been in my career.

The first day in this new role, I began building relationships. The athletics department faced major challenges, and I was tasked with developing and implementing much of the change. I began by mounting a social campaign to build trust and accountability within the department. I also volunteered to serve on nine different university committees, enrolled in several citywide leadership programs, served on multiple nonprofit boards and attended every student event on campus. I established solid relationships with the university president, board members, vice presidents, deans, the provost, unit directors and faculty.

My first two years in the position, I probably worked 60-plus hours a week. In addition, I enrolled in a doctoral program. This was what competing looked like. I pushed myself in ways I never imagined possible. Looking back, I realize I wasn't very healthy. I was exhausted all the time and ignored my physical and mental health. Still, I understood the significance of this opportunity.

I led a comprehensive transformation of Academic Support Services and Champs/Life Skills units. My tenure resulted in the highest Academic Progress Rate (APR) rankings in the history of men's basketball (1,000 APR rate for three consecutive years); an 80 percent graduation rate for African-American males who played football, and a cumulative student-athlete GPA of 3.0 for five straight years. At the time, the academic center became known as a "best practice" department at the university.

In addition, I implemented a $1.8 million Title IX Gender Equity plan that aligned female/male coaching salaries, increased scholarship and travel allocations, professional development, fundraising initiatives and a marketing infrastructure to support women's sports programs. The plan resulted in a 100 percent increase in revenues, ticket sales, fundraising and community outreach. Under my leadership, the university was ranked number one and recognized by USA Today for hiring the highest percentage of female coaches for female sport teams.

In just four years, the entire administrative team and Department of Athletics had recorded the most successes in the history of the program. This included an increase in overall team winning percentages, academic accolades, awards and community service hours. The department was highly successful, and I was delighted to be a part of all the success.

Unlike my prior experiences, I worked hard to build an extended internal and external network to help advance my personal and professional agenda. By the end of my third year at the university, I was known as a highly competent, trusted and well-respected employee. In the department, I became known as the go-to person. I received several promotions.

While I enjoyed the fruits of my labor, not every experience translated into a high-five moment or promotion. When you're the SWA, danger is ever-present. For example, when I recommended a salary increase for the women's track coach, and not the men's coach, the male athletic director expressed deep concerns for the male coach. He said that the increase could create an inequitable financial balance for the male coach and questioned the legality of the salary difference. I acknowledged his concerns and provided a comprehensive rationale for my recommendation, citing the women's team's recent competitive success, its larger student-athlete roster and its participation in both indoor and outdoor seasons. These factors resulted in more athletic contests, a bigger staff and more managerial duties and responsibilities. At the time, the men's team had fewer student-athletes and a smaller staff and did not field an indoor team, which reduced the number of its competitive events. I assured the athletics director that the salary increase could be justified based on the female coach's expanded managerial role and additional responsibilities.

Despite my evidence, I could see that he was still perplexed by the request and my insistence to move forward with the increase. So I immediately asked a dangerous question. I asked whether he had similar concerns about the unequal pay for the men's basketball coach, who earned three times the salary of the women's basketball coach. He abruptly ended our meeting after asking me to double-check the budget request with legal counsel, the Human Resources Department and the finance director before we moved forward. It took more than two months from that meeting to get the raise approved.

After battling to increase funding, salaries, advertising and support for the women's programs, I found myself facing a similar battle. I had received a promotion and title change, but no salary increase. My promotion was part of a comprehensive restructuring plan designed to streamline reporting processes and publicly acknowledge and reward the contributions of high-performing employees. It included five employees.

At the time of the promotion, my supervisor acknowledged my accomplishments, changed my title and expressed deep regret that the promotion did not come with additional compensation because of looming departmental budget constraints. As a senior-level administrator, I had firsthand knowledge of the department's budget problems, so I didn't push the issue at the time.

Six months after the promotion, though, I was contacted by a few search firms about other job opportunities. I updated my resume, conducted a compensation analysis to see how my salary compared to other administrators with similar job titles and responsibilities, and contacted my professional networks. I learned through the compensation analysis that my male counterparts with the same or lesser-ranking titles with fewer responsibilities received higher salaries than mine. I also learned that, of the five employees promoted earlier in the year, I was the only person who had not received additional compensation.

Stunned by the apparent disparities, I requested a meeting to discuss my concerns and outline a plan to reconcile the matter. Weeks passed as the administration avoided my request for a meeting. Nevertheless, I persisted.

Once we were in the meeting, my direct supervisor immediately denied my request for equal compensation. He dismissed the notion that I was underpaid and even expressed a hint of disgust in my "selfish" actions to request a higher salary given the departmental budget constraints.

I pushed back and highlighted that we had just renegotiated a higher salary for a male coach. Once again, my gift of questioning and my eyes-wide-open tricks were dangerous. I'm sure my questions and actions were viewed as a form of insubordination, so he dug in, reaffirmed his stance and left me with a veiled threat. *"This matter is over," he said. "You can always file an official complaint with the Office of Equal Opportunity or Human Resources."*

For many employees, filing an official complaint against a department and university is an enormous and dangerous proposition. It brings fears of retaliation, limited future career opportunities, poor evaluations or recommendations, along with negative exposure. I'm no different. I knew what was at stake. I spent days debating, consulting with experts and getting legal advice from top officials about my chances of resolving the issue.

Then I had an "Esther" moment. How could I fight for others and not be willing to fight for myself? So I sent the following email to the university's director of equal opportunity:

After reflecting on our meeting Friday and the way in which I have been blatantly excluded, I am requesting this matter be fully investigated. In addition, I'm requesting a full equity review of my position and ask the university to consider back pay for those months in which (I believe) my department administrators consciously withheld my official title change so that I would not receive proper compensation. This has obviously been a difficult situation for me. The idea that I have been treated differently breaks down my trust for those in leadership. More importantly, my silence in this matter only continues to promote an environment that has not been equitable and, in my mind, is discriminatory. While I understand the potential internal consequences for this decision, the perpetuating consequences bear a bigger price. Please let me know how I should proceed. Thanks in advance.

My experiences as an SWA taught me that the demand for equality and justice begins at home. It is disingenuous to fight for others and not advocate on your own behalf. Leadership starts with the leader, and when we fail to uphold our own values, principles and beliefs in justice due to fear, we also diminish our own capacity to fight for others.

Overtime, I've also come to believe that women, minorities and others who face similar conditions have a greater responsibility to ensure that their personal rights and the rights of others are secure. While it is certainly easier to accept the current conditions and play alone, we must acknowledge the weighty burden we leave for others if we remain silent. And while I'm clear that we certainly cannot fight every battle or take on every cause, every once in a while, in our careers, we have a sense of the weight and consequences of both our actions and inactions. It is in these times that true leaders take a stand.

Journal Entry #6: Taking A Stand

1. Describe an "Esther" moment in your life, whether at home, in public or at work, when you used your privilege, power and responsibility to change the outcome.

2. What thought process led you to act?

3. How did the incident change you?

6

ATHLETICS: TOO MUCH FOR THEIR TOO LITTLE

Wanna fly, you got to give up the
shit that weighs you down.

—*Toni Morrison, "Song of Solomon," 1977*

As a result of the department's success, my supervisor received a more lucrative job offer at another university and took it. Six months later, a new director of athletics was hired. My initial impression was positive. He seemed nice, trustworthy and sincere. Within months of his arrival, I was promoted and given a title change. He seemed impressed with my broad network and knowledge of the department.

But things quickly changed after I witnessed and protested the termination of two minority male employees in the department. While the specifics of each case held varying degrees of merit, the true conflict stemmed from the dynamics that played out between us, both in front of coaches and with the president of the university, who was one of my staunchest allies.

While it was natural for our coaching staff to see me as a trusted ally because of my long tenure and track record of directness and honesty, my supervisor bristled at the deference staff showed me. The same held true in interactions with the university president, who unwittingly added kindling to the flame of resentment I felt growing toward me when he openly and clearly sought my opinion about an athletic department conflict.

Though I dutifully followed my boss's directives, I never did so without asking questions I felt were critically important. I stepped in and out of roles and responsibilities to support the departmental team without complaint. Nevertheless, when I was called in to several meetings after the minority employees were terminated, I could see the road ahead of me once more.

The punishment for my protest was swift. As a seasoned administrator, I recognized all the signs, tactics and verbiage used to extinguish unwanted employees in the organization. In this case, my eyes-always-open trick helped me prepare for my own battle.

All the meetings started the same—with a string of compliments on my work ethic, professionalism and influence in the community. So, I started listening for what I didn't hear. My supervisor took great pleasure in reminding me of my recent promotion, his support and approval of my attending a prestigious leadership development program, the importance of showing gratitude and finally, his demand that I support all decisions in the department. Like a good employee, I sincerely thanked him for the recent promotion and the professional development opportunity and reaffirmed my loyalty to his vision for the department.

Despite my heartfelt sentiment, his ego seemed challenged by the fact that I would dare express concern and dissent regarding the disparate treatment of two minority employees. Looking back, I now believe those meetings served two purposes—they gave the appearance of support while they attempted to extinguish any opposing ideas I might have. Each time, I was reminded that even the slightest disagreement, even if my opinion was solicited, was viewed as dangerous discourse. It was a familiar message, subtle but clear: "Shut up, stay in your place, and be thankful you are working here."

These messages were of particular concern given my long and successful tenure at the university. Up until these encounters, my accomplishments at the university included promotions, title changes, financial compensation and national leadership recognitions.

From all accounts, I was highly competent, a top performer in the organization and viewed as a trusted resource for the university president, deans and other key community stakeholders. Then, out of nowhere, the university's first African-American president, my closest ally, resigned from the university. And, within 48 hours of his resignation, I was summoned into more meetings.

I share this seemingly unrelated coincidence because on their face, the two events—the president's resignation and the march toward my administrative leave— seem unrelated. However, I contend that the collective survival of minorities is often dependent upon the individual survival of other Black and Brown administrators and faculty.

In the meetings, I was accused of not having the psychological aptitude to be objective in my views regarding people of color and described as not being a good team player. I was accused of making people in the department feel uncomfortable or threatened by my leadership style. Ultimately, I was being portrayed as the angry Black woman.

As I struggled to reconcile their accusations with my reality, I began to forward sensitive emails and journal entries (Thoughts of the Day) to a personal email account. In response to the initial harsh critique, I needed to remind myself of who I was. I needed to find comfort in my own remembrance of self, so I wrote the following poem:

I'm not who you say I am.
I'm more.
I'm not an untrustworthy person
I am the person who tells my uncanny truth and expects others to do the same.
I'm not a person who is easily persuaded by the crowd.
I am a woman who stands for her convictions, willing to take the pain and the rewards.
I'm not a coward who throws rocks behind a person's back and smiles in their face.
I am a woman who shows the rock, tries to prevent from throwing, and lets you know it's coming.
I am not this Black thing you make me out to be.
I am a human being—a person full of color and spirit.
I am the Goddess of this nation. I am the purified love of God. I
AM.

In an attempt to self-soothe, the poem was a desperate attempt at affirming that my hard work, education and ethical value system would somehow thwart what I sensed was happening. I began to reinvent myself, work harder and create new initiatives. Determined to prove my loyalty and secure my job, I put in more hours. I was determined to overachieve and outwork everyone on the team. Days later, I was called into yet another meeting. After the meeting, I wrote:

> *He stated repeatedly that I am always professional and outworked the executive staff members; however, he felt like I was not "all in." I reminded him of all the new initiatives I had taken on in the past month. I asked him why he felt that way. He could not give me an answer. I asked him how I could be better or what he needed from me to ensure him I was on board. Seemingly shocked by my question, he replied that he did not know.*

I remember leaving this particular meeting with a greater understanding that this was not about me but rather about his inner feelings of inadequacy. I was appalled by his lack of clarity or specifics about what I needed to change. It wasn't until I asked for a specific example that I got the real answer…nothing. Nothing was the threat. Insubordination or failing to do my job are easy answers, but "you make me feel inadequate and uncomfortable in my own skin" is not an acceptable answer. Instead, I understood it as a sanitized expression of race and gender prejudice.

I started suffering bouts of anxiety, despair and anger. My daily "Thoughts of the Day" became personal therapy. As the only Black female executive in the department, the isolation was unbearable.

I needed to purge my soul without compromising my professional integrity. I could feel the anger roaring in my belly, so I continued to self-soothe, empower and educate myself through journaling.

I wrote:

> *Controlling one's emotions and playing the game is the most important aspect of leading. I listened as people talked about Linda's calming nature. I wonder if she was calm outwardly, yet suffering internally. How do you balance the two without feeling like a fake? I struggle with confronting my attackers. As a Black woman, my actions are always judged as aggressive. The balance is not to appear aggressive, yet be aggressive. I need to do a better job at playing the game and not allowing my emotions to play for me. While this is difficult, it is the ultimate battle. I absolutely don't trust anyone in the athletics department. I'm alone on this island, yet they are more than willing to use my talents.*
>
> *Once people show you themselves, believe them. He has shown himself. Believe him, and keep it moving. Knowing where you stand is empowering; reacting to the knowledge is weak. I must not react to my place in the organization but rather understand it and use the power of knowing. You hold all the cards by understanding your place and not fearing or resenting the process through which you find yourself. Don't panic or fight in the midst of confrontation. Battles are often won outside of the rink.*

Then it happened; I was called into the final meeting. As was the case in most of the meetings, I was assaulted by questions and required to regurgitate my concerns about my colleagues' terminations as well as to affirm my support of the AD's ability to lead the department. I faced repeated and clarifying questions designed to confuse and to test my knowledge of truth. I believed the conversations were being recorded.

Exhausted, I simply asked once again, "What do you need from me?" Unlike previous conversations, the AD appeared ready for the question this time. As if he were reading from a prepared statement, he gently requested my submission to him and the others in the department. He alluded that he and others were intimidated and threatened by my presence, and if I wanted to remain a part of the team, I needed to change.

After 90 minutes of interrogation, no real examples of misconduct and a tempered request to be submissive, I gave up. I simply threw in the towel and promised to be "better," despite not having a clear sense of what "being better" meant. I was shattered and didn't have the strength to fight this system anymore.

The next morning, I woke with a start at 3 a.m., grabbed my computer, and began to write a "Thought of the Day." In that moment, my body, mind and soul needed to purge. Before dawn, I had written a two-page, single-spaced response to my supervisor detailing the dreadful proceedings of the past two months; and I requested a follow-up meeting. This was another Gladys' trial moment, and I was prepared once again to advocate for myself. Here is a portion of my defense:

During our last two conversations, I have asked repeatedly for specific examples in which I have displayed inappropriate or intimidating behaviors to any colleagues. You have failed to give me one example. After our two talks, I always leave the meeting feeling as if I have done something wrong, yet you never bring any concrete examples from which I can work to get better. Yesterday was no different. You talked about how I bring a high level of critical thinking to the table, how important I am to the team's success and how the others look up to me. In most organizations, those would be good things. Yet, somehow, I leave the meeting feeling like a failure with no direction. While you might dismiss that race, stature and gender play a role in this, they do. Deep in my heart, I feel you have a level of frustration because I have not appeared to be "humbled enough."

I continued…

After careful thought and another sleepless night, I have come to the conclusion that this is about diversity and leadership. This is about being different, thinking different, leading different. These issues derive from unconscious and conscious racial fears of something that might happen, yet never does.

I am not willing to diminish my role as a leader because others feel inadequate. I am passionate, humble, strong-willed, opinionated, Black, female and tall. That's who I am. If you feel I add value to this team, then the decision is not whether Robin should be on the team or how she can make others feel safe but rather, how you lead this collective team to be better. While I am not blameless in this entire situation, I am also not the cause of the problem. I am just an easy way out to avoid the difficult conversation about race, gender and leadership.

At the end of the day, you have all the power. You have the power, not me, to change this culture. You have an opportunity to lead this group. I've prayed about this entire situation; I've turned it over to God. What happens next is left on the altar, not with me and not with you. I forgive you, and I forgive myself. I will move forward to making the best of this situation and being the best professional for the department. That's all I have to give.

After reading the letter, I knew instinctively that my tenure in the department would end soon. I could see the anger in his response to the meeting. With disgust in his eyes, I'm sure he was thinking—how dare I have the unmitigated gall to confront the issue head-on. How dare I come in the meeting with a prepared statement, facts and questions about his authority and capacity.

Ten days later, early Saturday morning as I worked on another project, I received a formal email from the interim chief general counsel advising me that I had been placed on a two-week paid administrative leave for "what appears to be a breakdown in communications resulting in what may be a total loss of trust between you and the boss."

Given the sensitive legal matter, I cannot share the entire document. However, I was astonished by the lack of professionalism with which the university handled this entire situation. Prior to receiving this letter, I had no communication with anyone. I was not contacted by Human Resources, the president, legal counsel or anyone in the department to discuss the cause of the "breakdown in communication."

Ironically, the salutation used at the end of the memo read: "Regards." This letter and the entire incident demonstrated a total lack of regard. No one regarded my story, my narrative and my concerns about the matter prior to receiving this letter. And now, "regards." Despite having a longer tenure, a clean HR file and a respected reputation at the university, I quickly learned who had the privilege of telling stories and who did not. My outstanding evaluations, multiple promotions and enormous workload couldn't prevent this mindless game. He complained I was a problem; therefore, I was a problem.

I was astonished by the ease with which my body and career could be deposed. I scheduled meetings with general counsel, requested a meeting with the president and sent notice to other Black faculty and administrators about my recent employment status. Then I waited for a response.

Most hurtful was seeing the names of two Black women included on the memo. While I don't believe either Black employee had the power or played a significant role in my dismissal, the cosigning reference of Blacks and minorities is a commonly used tactic to dispel any notion of racial or sexist misconduct. In this case, the attorney strategically referenced the two Black women to justify the discriminatory actions by ensuring other Blacks were in agreement and culpable in the assault. As Sam Greenlee points out in "The Spook Who Sat by the Door," other Black and Brown employees are often used as scapegoats and pawns in the deadly game of racial roulette.

Less than 48 hours after I was placed on administrative leave, the interim chief general counsel and a newly hired lawyer scheduled a follow-up meeting. Unlike others at the university, I could recognize all the signs and tactics used to rid the institution of people like me. I had seen the war; my professional experiences privileged me in ways I couldn't ever imagine. This was another Slapping Becky moment, and I was prepared to defend myself.

The meeting lasted about 90 minutes. I did most of the talking. After the hearty discussion, I'm sure the thought of a legal battle inspired the university to create a new position and relocate me to another department. Ironically, I was placed in a diversity and inclusion role. Three days later, I signed a new contract, received an insignificant pay increase and moved into another building. A 13-year successful career was destroyed by an insecure administrator and the university's failure to conduct a simple investigation.

Leaving athletics was bittersweet—bitter in the way it ended, yet sweetened by a new career path. Truth be told, I needed to leave athletics. It was time. I had served my purpose and completed my mission, but I didn't have the courage to leave. This life-altering event changed and redefined my personal and professional career; it transformed me in ways I never imagined.

So I wrote:

> *People watch you because you are special. Give them something special to watch. Don't allow this moment in time to change your core values or your spirit. Continue to live the life God has blessed you with, and continue to pray for everyone involved. Forgiveness or dwelling on the*

> *negative only takes away from our individual God-given talents and the blessings in our lives. This place is only a moment in time. Don't give this moment any more time.*

This experience taught me that good employees sometimes lose great jobs because of ineffective employers. While I can sugarcoat the message, the saying—good people don't leave organizations; they leave bad bosses—is true. Sometimes we lose jobs not because of underperformance. Sometimes it's because we outperform the people around us and make them feel insecure. I wish someone had told me earlier that there are moments when we are "too much" for other people's "too little," because, throughout my career, I spent too much time trying to make others feel comfortable and safe and changed who I was—just to feel normal.

In addition, I learned that the narrator of the story controls the script, the characters and in some cases, the story's ending. People in power know that. It is the one uninterrogated, powerful and deadly tool in the tool kit. The statement—he said I was a problem; therefore, I was a problem—demonstrates the powerful nature of storytelling narratives. It also demonstrates the need for leaders to keep their eyes open, ask more questions, and ensure that every person is heard.

Finally, I learned that the lack of diversity in the workplace and the perpetual failures of people of color cannot simply be explained using the ideology of intellectual inferiority—he/she was not a "good fit," or that it just didn't work out. In some cases, the failure lies in the racial and cultural ignorance of a heavily white administration and faculty, and it should be examined not as a byproduct of happenstance but as strategy.

Journal Entry #7: Wanna Fly?

Respond to the following quote: *"Wanna fly, you got to give up the shit that weighs you down."*

1. What is weighing you down? What must you give up, to achieve your goal?

2, If you were not afraid, what would you do? Be specific and provide details of what you would accomplish if you led beyond the fear.

PART 3

Diversity, Inclusion and Higher Education

7

DIVERSITY: UPWARD TRAJECTORY UPENDED

As long as we are not ourselves, we will try to be what other people are.

—Malidoma Patrice Somé, "Of Water and the Spirit," 1994

With no time to reflect or heal, one week after leaving my position in athletics, I was appointed as the associate provost for diversity and inclusion. I was no longer on administrative leave. Instead, I had been elevated into a position in the office charged with daily academic operations across the entire university. Excited about the opportunity, I was determined to prove myself, so I hit the ground running.

Colleagues and friends commented on my positive attitude and praised the grace with which I handled the entire transition. As a Black woman, I had witnessed and combated this level of personal assault before. Somewhere deep down, I had become programmed to anticipate this kind of harsh reality and knew how to keep it moving.

In my first week in the new position, I was offered and graciously accepted random invitations to lunch with new colleagues. While I'm sure my colleagues had good intentions, the lunch meetings felt like dog-sniffing ceremonies. It was a time to sniff around for any abnormalities, hints of anger or laziness. Time to assess my friendliness and gauge if I would be a "good" team member. Since I had spent years building strong relationships throughout our community, my lunch meetings often turned into a parade of greetings and well wishes as people stopped to congratulate me on my promotion. My positive public persona, along with my big smile and delectable New Orleans–style red beans and rice recipe, eased the minds and alleviated concerns people might have had about me.

As a highly intelligent Black woman, I don't pretend to be an innocent victim or bystander in the workplace. I know how to sharpen my claws and fight when I need to. Still, the fear of having to find another job, along with the fear of being labeled the angry Black woman, haunted me. I was determined to use what control I had to create my own positive narrative about how blessed and grateful I was for this new and unexpected opportunity.

I sent the following email to my new supervisor and colleagues:

> *Just wanted to say thanks for the opportunity and support. I am truly grateful. I am fully onboard in making this university a better place for everyone. I am also dedicated to seeing my transition is done with class and professionalism. I've enjoyed my former career, but I am*

passionately excited about this new career path. Thanks again for everything.

I sent this message to my university colleagues:

Hey everyone,

Yesterday I joined (new supervisor's) team as (position title). I'm extremely excited about my new role in the university. Just wanted to say thanks for all your support and prayers. I will certainly need both as I move forward in my new role. Thanks again.

Hey,

Hope all is well. Didn't know if you heard…I accepted a new position and started today. I am soooooo excited to work with (new supervisor). This new role aligns with my dissertation studies and future aspirations of becoming a university president. Let's connect soon.

I used these emails as a tool to write my own new narrative. How else do you explain what you cannot explain? You feel the pain, you relive the daily assaults, and you try to find words to adequately articulate the emotions. But you can't. It's too much. The stories are too long. They incriminate too many people; maybe even you.

On the surface, everything looked great—a new job, an anemic raise in salary and the opportunity to start over. Others would argue that the system worked—good prevailed, and merit was rewarded. I was held up like a beacon of hope, a shining example of liberal morality.

I had turned lemons into lemonade. And so I started to do what I did best—work my ass off.

In this newly created position, I began to define, create and implement new programs and initiatives that directly increased faculty diversity and inclusive practices. I helped design and manage a comprehensive executive leadership curriculum to advance women faculty and staff who aspired to senior academic and administrative positions; I managed a faculty Strategic Hiring and Dual Career program that doubled the number of underrepresented faculty hired at the university; and I managed the largest middle and high school science fair in the region. I said yes to every new task or job assignment. A few of my key accomplishments were even featured in *The Journal of Blacks in Higher Education*.

More Carnage

I had not fully settled into my new role before realizing that another person of color was headed down the dark, perilous road of being a Black administrator in higher education. As the university's only African-American dean, he was openly attacked by high-ranking administrators who questioned his abilities and demonstrated a total lack of respect for his authority. I was copied on an email from a senior administrator who referred to him as a "trash distractor." I watched how a select group of faculty bullied, oppressed and publicly emasculated the university's president, the minority dean and other faculty members, all while hiding behind the privileged veil of academic freedom.

In this particular case, bogus email accounts, anonymous blogs, a letter to the local newspaper and racist posters replaced intellectual discussions. Technology was used like an assault weapon—it allowed some faculty to vanish behind the obscure protection of tenure, research and union contracts as they ruled with an iron fist. I remember leaving my beautiful office, hiding behind a building, as I stood to read devastating messages decrying the dean's every move. I remember weeping quietly, and then 30 minutes later, drying my eyes and walking back to my office, all the while pretending like nothing had happened.

Then it occurred to me, that one key prevailing, and often forgotten travesty that accompanies these firings and administrative leave decisions is the collective toll it takes on Black families, their health and personal and professional relationships. I saw it happen to me. Sure, I received a few cards, bouquets of flowers and well wishes, but at the end of the day, from the very first day, everyone, including me, just moved on.

When I left athletics, my friends and colleagues didn't know how to help me. They watched from afar, they offered support, and then they turned the other way. This is far from judgment because I've done the very same. Every time a Black person was terminated or demoted, I instinctively wondered how I could have, or should have, done more. In some cases, I took action, and in others, I gave a half-assed effort.

Each time I saw another colleague's upward trajectory inverted, I questioned the decisions and returned to my corner office feeling more isolated. While some see these things as normal ways of doing business, every time it happens, we all become desensitized by the deadly carnage. We come to accept it. It's not until we are faced with the same set of circumstances that we become indignant about what is happening. To this day, I often question my personal and professional failures in this area.

The entire incident with the dean reopened personal wounds from athletics that I had thought were healed. I began to struggle and faced periods of self-doubt. I perpetually interrogated myself: *Was I in the wrong? Was I really not good enough? Did I deserve the mistreatment because of some real or imagined flaw?* I found myself constantly reflecting and replaying my entire career in search of answers. This destructive survival strategy of constant self-reflection, both consumed and undermined my personal worth. Consciously or unconsciously, I started avoiding any potential conflict that would result in negative emotions or outcomes. I called this TENDing.

TENDing means Trying to Erase the Needs and Dilemmas of others. I started using it as a term to describe times when I felt the need to ease or tend to the emotional needs of white colleagues with whom I disagreed, or whom I offended or made feel uncomfortable. As an African-American woman serving in executive leadership positions, I can't even count the number of hours I've spent consoling, cajoling and reassuring white colleagues that I am not mad or angry, and that they should feel safe around me. It is exhausting.

While some of this might be a result of my physical stature as a 6-foot, 3-inch tall woman, often it stems from my distinctive and often contrary point of view. While I believe that self-actualization and self-reflection are critical competencies for great leaders, as a Black woman, I'm frequently reminded to reflect more often, to modify my tone or body language, to adjust my level of input (too much or too little) or to temper my passion. These constant demands for self-reflection and obsessive analyses of my every action are consuming, undermining and destructive.

In my new provost office role, TENDing became a top priority. I was adamant: I would no longer be labeled the angry Black woman. My actions started to resemble the Mammy archetype described in Melissa Harris-Perry's "Sister Citizen": I was the trusted advisor and confidante, nonthreatening and nurturing. Not only that, I was expected to tend to the needs of others. Somewhere along the way, my contentious exit from athletics inspired me to make this dramatic, and problematic, attitude shift.

Despite the negative connotations associated with the Mammy archetype, my TENDing efforts produced positive results. I was well liked, invited to special events, nominated for prestigious awards and selected for community boards. I was recognized as a helpful, trusted adviser and confidante. As long as I played the Mammy role, everything and everyone around me seemed fine.

However, I eventually came to realize that the Mammy mask should come with a cautionary note that reads: This mask is easy to get on, but difficult to remove. A year into my tenure, colleagues had already come to expect to be TENDed to at all times. As a Black woman, I quickly learned that any slight variations in attitude or variations in tending activities, such as refusal to serve on a committee, failing to volunteer or simply expressing a staunch opinion on a contentious topic, often alters public opinion as to whether you are a "good fit" or team player.

As my TENDing activities and job responsibilities continued to expand, they began to take a physical and spiritual toll. Somewhere deep down inside, I knew it was time to stop TENDing and leave the Mammy archetype behind. In that moment, I finally understood that the experience in athletics had changed me. Maybe this was the goal of my former supervisor when he requested I become "more submissive" to my colleagues. Maybe he was asking me to be more like Mammy. And though I left athletics in defiance of many of those expectations that come along with TENDing, I never expected to craft that role for myself in the next chapter of my professional life. I write this not in judgment of the archetypal Mammy or the ancestors and professionals who TEND to survive or even just to keep their jobs. For me, though, TENDing made the real me once again invisible, even to myself. It was the first time in my life that I failed to self-advocate and believe in myself.

TENDing led me to reflect on the many leadership team meetings, retreats, even one-on-one strategic conversations, which often present me with the same personal and professional dilemmas. On one hand, my wise counsel, advice and tactical thinking skills are lauded and in demand. Conversely, too much wise counsel can quickly be described as disruptive. So while my mastery of the art of questioning will always get me a seat at the decision-making table, I'm rarely expected or encouraged to contribute in any substantive way. Put another way, I've learned that all people say they don't like the status quo, right up until it demands some sort of real change. Once change is inevitable, people will most likely fight to keep the very thing they claim to detest. This has always been a fascinating paradox to me, especially as a woman of color who is often hired to assist in managing change by fixing problems and cleaning up messes others have left behind.

Thought of the Day

Sometimes I/we wear the mask because people ask or demand that I/we do. Sometimes I/we wear the mask for protection or ease. I/we even wear it to be unseen. It covers the pain, the scars and hurts hiding both on the surface as well as scars so deep, they escape our memory. The mask is just that, a mask. The mask is a costume. It is the denial of our very existence and our humanity.

Journal Entry #8: Take the Mask Off

1. If the mask was off, what would people see?

2. If the mask was off, what do you want people to see?

8

INCLUDED--THE WORLD IS COLLAPSING, AND SO AM I

Many and most moments go by with us hardly aware of their passage. But love and hate and fear cause time to snag you, to drag you down like a spider's web holding fast to a doomed fly's wings.

—Walter Mosley, "When the Thrill Is Gone," 2011

It was 2015, and as if I were watching a series of horror films, the world seemed to erupt with violence as videos surfaced of Black and Brown men, women and children being murdered by police. Devastated by the civil unrest in the country, I struggled to find my personal and professional meaning.

It was like the universe was trying to get my attention, and I didn't want to listen. After leaving athletics, I just wanted to be invisible. I was tired and depleted and simply didn't have the physical or mental strength to fight more battles. However, once again, fate would grab hold of my spirit and twist my heart until it felt faint. I received an email from a former employee informing me that a former student-athlete whom I knew very well had recently been arrested while he was headed home after a university event. The charge against him was trespassing at a local gas station, resisting arrest and attempting to assault an officer. The student-athlete— along with a video recording from a bystander—told a different version of the incident.

Fearing an unfavorable outcome from what appeared to be a lopsided local justice system, the former employee called to seek my advice and assistance. I decided to take this on. I knew this young man. He was a good person and a talented athlete. Years prior to the incident, I had refused to renew his athletic scholarship because of his poor academic performance, only to reinstate him because of a clerical error. After his reinstatement on the team, he got his act together, graduated, and went on to become an All-American athlete. He was probably the best clerical mistake I ever made.

I jumped right into action. Using my positional, political and social influence in the community, I made several calls to report and express my disgust and dismay at the treatment of not only this young man in particular but also other Blacks who might be impacted by the university's policies and near-campus police practices. As a member of the Presidential Diversity Council and in my role in athletics, I had become critically aware of regular email notices of crimes around campus, which generally described suspects as 5-foot-9-inch Black males wearing hoodies—in short, nearly every Black student-athlete.

I called a member of our board of trustees, our vice president for student affairs, our chief diversity officer and a local city councilwoman to express my concerns about this particular incident. I also raised my objections to the increase in security and what appeared to be racial profiling tactics recently approved by the university president. As my pleas and warnings fell on mostly deaf ears, I turned to the only real possible resolution. I contacted a lawyer and paid a portion of the young man's legal fees. Neither my former employee, the alumnus, nor I had confidence in the public defender's capacity to advocate for a fair trial. Five painful months later, the student agreed to accept a plea deal, and with it a temporary stain on his record, just so he could move on.

After the deal, I asked the young man what he had learned. He replied: "I need to be more careful and go straight home after events, drive on main highways, not back streets and be more careful if I decide to hang out." He then talked about his two young children and how he planned to go to work, come straight home and take care of his family. I sat in silence and horror. Once again, like the movie *The Butler*, this experience had taught the student-athlete that society didn't *"even want to hear him breathe and the room should feel empty when he was in it."* He had learned how not to be free. The entire experience changed him. It changed his former coach. It changed me.

The horror stuck with me long after the incident. I talked with other university administrators and community leaders about what happened to our alumnus and how others might be impacted. Many insisted this was an isolated case; they assured me that protecting the university from crime and criminals was a top priority for the new campus leadership. I noted that the alumnus had never been considered a "criminal" before he was stopped. He had no prior police record, no signs of criminal behavior and yet in a matter of moments and without trial or jury, the holder of a Bachelor of Arts degree in criminal justice had been deemed a danger to the community and a part of the threatening criminal element.

As a Black female who grew up in the projects, I had firsthand knowledge about fear of the police, not to mention the dangers of just being Black in certain situations. I have friends, family and loved ones who have experienced the dangers of police violence. My doctoral degree, my well-paying job and even the plush trappings of my sleek corner office could not erase those experiences as an integral part of my reality. I felt things differently. I saw things differently; and therefore, I reacted differently.

This entire incident weakened me. Once again, I tried to reconcile my anguish by writing about it and telling my stories. I needed to purge, to share the story that wasn't being told anywhere else. I decided to write and publish the following opinion column in our local newspaper. It took three months, and the death of Freddy Gray, for me to write these words:

> *These days, I can't sleep. I wake suddenly with the image seared into my brain: a 25-year-old Black man handcuffed, shackled and allegedly given a "rough ride" in the back of a police car until his spine was severed.*
>
> *Sweaty, confused, angry and scared, I turn on the TV, look at the local news and start reading my recent Twitter feed in search of calm, of understanding. But instead, this is what I see:*
>
> *Q: "Did you hear about the Black man killed by police this month?"*

A: "Walter Scott, shot eight times in the back in Charleston?"

Q: "No, the other one."

A: "You mean 17-year-old Justus Howell, who was shot twice in the back outside Chicago three hours after Walter Scott was murdered?"

Q: "No, the other one."

A: "Philip White in New Jersey, whose face was chewed off by a K-9? He bled to death while officers tried to seize video evidence from witnesses?"

Q: "No, the other one."

A: "Eric Harris from Tulsa, who screamed, 'Oh my God, I'm losing my breath,' after being shot in the back, to which the commanding officer responded, 'F*** your breath?'"

Q: "No, the other one."

A: "Freddie Gray from Baltimore, who so far seems to have committed no crime other than catching the eye of a police officer, who while in custody somehow managed to have his spine severed in three places as his voice box collapsed? The neighborhood jokester who died in agony seven days later?"

What kind of blindness doesn't see the irony of Gray's lethal injuries occurring in the back of an official vehicle that reads "To Serve and Protect?"

That vision haunted me as I read more about Gray. I wish I could let those visions and that pain go, but I can't. It's like a life force calling me to respond, come forth and speak. While the case remains under investigation, the result is the same—another incapacitated person fatally injured while in the custody of those responsible for protecting and serving us all.

To be clear, I respect the police. I respect teachers, priests, governmental officials and firefighters. They have tough jobs. When you deal with people, much less people in stressful situations, it is sometimes unpredictable, dangerous and often thankless. Nevertheless, that reality does not excuse criminal behavior and its legal consequences. Or it shouldn't.

In fact, when these cases happen, they put all police officers, community leaders, teachers and even our legal system in harm's way. They make good officers suspects, untrustworthy and more importantly, hated. They lead other citizens to question whether their skin color or socio-economic status precludes them from accessing their inalienable rights, which can trigger aggressiveness, fear and anxiety. At least that's how I've been feeling lately.

The events of the past six months have sparked an international outcry as feelings of distress, fear, helplessness, anger, abandonment and horror plague millions of mothers now forced to deliver the "assume the position talk" of how to interact with the police to their children. This life-altering yet essential training leaves an entire community emotionally, physically and psychologically scarred. Feelings of inexplicable fear and sadness simply take our breath way—#icantbreathe.

For those of you who do not know the speech, it goes like this: *"Keep your hands in plain sight at all times. Keep your head down. Don't make any sudden moves, even if you're asked for an ID... Remember, the goal is just to come home alive."*

What 12-year-old walks away from that conversation feeling protected and served? Why should such a conversation exist in a fair and just society? We live in a culture that condones mayhem, public drunkenness and the destruction of property after national championship games, yet harshly defends calling in the National Guard dressed in riot gear when citizens dare to protest the death of an unarmed man at the hands of our government.

Is this the country we aspire to? Is this the best we can do? I hope not.

> But I ask because we all need to speak against police brutality and this country's economic and political dependence on the prison-industrial complex. If not, our children and our children's children will bear witness that we silently stood by and allowed millions of poor people, people with mental illnesses and immigrants to suffer at the hands of our silence. Neither you nor I can simply say, as in the case of many whites of privilege, "I didn't own any slaves, so don't blame me."
>
> Dear friends, this is happening on our watch. We, and I mean the collective we, can no longer sit idle while millions of people cry out in fear, anger and helplessness. #BlackLivesMatter is not about racial identity; it is a simple reminder that humanity matters, even when the skin pigmentation is blessed with a darker hue. If we don't all stand together on this front, we will all have to face, together, a generation of angry, disenfranchised citizens who watched at the age of 12 as our silence gave way to a two-sided justice system that offers civic protections to some but not to others. And on that day, my friends, we will all awaken in a state of fear.

Just after the piece published, the next inevitable and unimaginable event happened. My university was thrust into the national and international spotlight after video emerged that showed a university police officer shooting a local citizen in the head during an off-campus traffic stop. The reason for the traffic stop was a missing front license plate. After the shooting, my soul was awakened from unconscious TENDing once and for all.

I was out of town at a conference when I learned about the shooting via Twitter. I later called a close friend of mine in the administration, who told me grave details about the shooting and then predicted that this would get messy for the university. I was in shock. I had so many questions, so many fears and so much anger.

Instinctively, my internal questions started: *Had the university implemented policies that unknowingly targeted Black and Brown citizens? Was the new university police chief hired to implement and manage what appeared to be a stop-and-frisk program? Did university police have legal authority to make off- campus traffic stops? Is it illegal not to have a front license plate on your car?*

These questions helped me connect more dots. My memory flooded with details of a joint agreement between university officials and the city's police force to expand security around campus in an attempt to rid the university of any "criminal elements" that might bring harm to students, faculty and staff.

As a member of the provost's senior staff, I had interviewed the then-candidates for police chief. I asked the candidate who got the job about crime and its impact on the local community. I was forceful and direct in my questioning when I asked him how he planned to protect both the community and the university. He responded with details about how to stop external criminal behavior; however, he provided little strategy to deal with illegal student and staff behavior on campus. I left that interview perplexed and livid. As I walked back to my office, I made small talk with a colleague and recorded the following personal note on my phone: "University police is now involved in locking up our kids" time stamped (Sept. 9, 2014, at 11 a.m.).

Months later, unable to escape the physical, psychological and spiritual anguish, I started to become angry. I had started to become the very thing I loathed and worked so hard to avoid. I could no longer pretend or TEND to the needs of others and witness more destruction.

On the surface, though, everything seemed fine. I had a great job. I was paid well. I worked on meaningful projects and got along well with the staff in the office. Still, I felt depleted. As a researcher, I recognized what was happening. I was experiencing what William Smith refers to as racial battle fatigue or the social-psychological effects of both personal and collective racialized trauma. My personal and professional experiences had begun to shape my identity and activities, causing a kind of physiological warfare. Suddenly, a simple walk from the garage toward my office left me filled with pain, disgust and shame. What had been a point of pride—an impressive role at a major research university—abruptly represented everything wrong in the world. Soon afterwards, I decided to leave the provost's office and accept a full-time faculty position, along with a significant pay cut.

When colleagues or friends asked why I gave up a lauded executive position and took a significant pay cut to become a faculty member, I had a predetermined response: "So I can become a college president someday." While being a college president is certainly one of my career aspirations, the explanation seemed more appropriate than expressing a deeper truth about the personal trauma I was experiencing daily.

Thought of the Day

When we see ourselves, we see others. Our sameness or collective interconnection is what unites us and demands justice for all. We have spent too much misguided energy and rhetoric on the idea of individual merit and earned accolades, so that we've forgotten our interdependence upon others—all others.

Journal Entry #9: The Moment of Shift

1. Describe a moment in which you experienced a shift in your personal and professional life. What was the outcome? Would you do anything differently today? Why or why not?

9

INSTITUTIONAL DIVERSITY GETS AN F

We are not fighting for integration, nor are we fighting for separation. We are fighting for recognition as human beings...In fact, we are actually fighting for rights that are even greater than civil rights, and that is human rights.

—Malcolm X, The Black Revolution speech, 1964

Universities are large, complex communities. In theory and in practice, I fully understand that the leadership, management and all stakeholders are simply unable to fully investigate every employee firing. There are no simple answers, reasons or justification as to why employees stay and why they leave, by choice or by force. I know from both sides that employee terminations are difficult, convoluted and often completed within a vacuum under the direction of a single direct supervisor.

Over the course of eight years working at a large research institution as a senior administrator, diversity officer and tenure-track faculty member, I witnessed the termination of many Black and Brown colleagues.

I saw a smart yet meek African-American woman devoured after simply following through on her boss's demands. When her compliance proved disastrous, her Black body and career were sacrificed. She negotiated a six-month severance, and the matter was buried without further inquiry.

I watched as they terminated a promising young Black male administrator after he attended a professional development conference but failed to properly record vacation time. On its face, his firing seemed justified; however, a simple stroll past empty offices and a quick cross-check of vacation notices would prove that this was a common practice within the department. Again, three months of salary, no questions, no investigation and no real effort to understand why this Black body was gone after only 12 months.

I watched as two men of color, both staff members, faced accusations of sexual misconduct. In the first sexual misconduct case, the alleged offenses were investigated, and university officials found neither grounds for termination nor any evidence of sexual misconduct. Nevertheless, the employee resigned under distress and given eight months of salary. Two months later, it was time to destroy that second Black body. This time, an administrator conducted his own investigation and only contacted the Human Resource department days after the termination. Just like the other employees, he was terminated without cause and asked to pack his belongings and exit the building immediately. His career trajectory has never been the same.

During the height of the exodus of more African-American administrators and faculty, two months after a university police officer shot and killed an unarmed Black man and after the university commissioned an independent report that showed a pattern of excessive and aggressive traffic stops of Blacks near campus, incredibly, the university received several national diversity awards and recognitions.

The university was recognized and selected by INSIGHT into Diversity magazine, one of the largest and oldest publications of its kind in higher education, as the winner of the Higher Education Excellence in Diversity (HEED) Award. This honor—the only national designation of its kind—acknowledges U.S. colleges and universities that demonstrate an outstanding commitment to diversity and inclusion. It's important to note that the university had received the honor the previous year.

At nearly the same time, the American Council on Education honored the university's president with the Reginald Wilson Diversity Leadership Award. This happened after a Black student group launched a national protest campaign and Black faculty members petitioned the board of trustees, highlighting disparate conditions for Black faculty and staff, as well as a decreased enrollment of African-American students.

The purpose of highlighting these national recognitions is not to condemn the American Council on Education or the Reginald Wilson Award committees. My point is to highlight the fact that organizations, institutions and diversity leaders rarely thoroughly interrogate institutions' treatment of Black and Brown professionals. If we fail to interrogate the system, we will also fail to interrogate the merits of accolades bestowed in the name of "inclusive excellence."

As a former associate provost for diversity and inclusion, I believe that, in its current structure, institutional Diversity with a capital D has little relevance. In fact, it often inadvertently marginalizes the very people it aims to protect. And having worked in the role and served on numerous diversity committees, I no longer trust fake diversity and inclusion initiatives that hide behind a mirage of special programs, awards and smiling faces.

This chapter stands as a direct critique of the ideology of meritocracy, which has come to represent the following misguided equation: hard work or "good" girl + a great education = economic, political and social parity and a solution to racism and sexism. The narratives throughout this book show how normalized racism is perpetuated and preserved by various actors in the academy, and how protest and dangerous discourse can lead to more racial disparity for Black and Brown administrators, faculty and staff—not less.

They illuminate the hypocrisy behind the academy's insidious love affair with the words *diversity* and *inclusion*, illustrating a lack of uncomfortable discourse about the ways institutional "diversity" initiatives lure people into believing that a single colorized person of power—the chief diversity officer—can erase the systemic racism that plagues academic institutions. On the contrary, the narratives reinforce the undeniable truth that advanced degrees and clean police records do not guarantee job security or protection against deeply rooted prejudices and discriminatory practices.

I share these stories as a way to purge and cleanse my digestive system of the venomous waste of so many unmet promises, and to call upon courageous outsiders to actively participate in the change. If Diversity and Inclusion efforts are to remain relevant, leaders must actively seek dangerous discourse, pursue multiple truths and rid university's reliance upon tangential diversity awards, simple programs and elaborate public announcements about diversity efforts. We must take a comprehensive look into the merits and value of diversity and inclusion, as well as acknowledge a system of violence upon Black and Brown bodies currently serving in institutions of higher education. Finally, we must scrutinize the role Diversity and Inclusion experts play in maintaining the deafening silence of minorities, as universities face a groundswell of racial and civil unrest.

In his critique of the American dream, "Between the World and Me," Ta-Nehisi Coates writes: "The Dream thrives on generalization, on limiting the number of possible questions, on privileging immediate answers. The Dream is the enemy of all art, courageous thinking and honest writing.[3]"

Now replace the word Dream with "institutional diversity and inclusion efforts in higher education," and see those efforts in a new light. In my experience, this surface work of diversity, equity and inclusion breeds simple answers, limits possible questions and allows uninterrogated decision-making by educational leaders who are rarely forced to recognize, much less embrace, the multidimensionality, complexity, honesty and boundary-spanning efforts required to create truly inclusive and equitable environments.

So I end this chapter with a call to educational scholars, administrators and staff alike to demand uncompromising inquiry into the policies, practices and increased political, social and media lip service paid to diversity and inclusion. It is time to expose and unmask racism

3 Ta-Nehisi Coates, *Between the World and Me*, first edition. (New York, NY: Spiegel & Grau, 2015), 50.

by engaging and encouraging dialogues outside of the typical, comfortable diversity and inclusion discourse. It is time for educational leaders to become, as Coates writes, "politically conscious," which he describes as a series of actions, as a state of being, and as a way of using questions as ritual, rather than any kind of search for certainty.

The kind of critical change that must happen isn't played out in front of spotlights. It requires self-sacrifice, the risk of alienation and rejection. Even, costly consequences. It will require more transformative leaders to use their authority and privilege to ask hard questions, knowing that there are no perfect or easy answers. Essentially, demands perseverance and understanding that building a successful path forward requires getting comfortable with being uncomfortable.

Journal Entry #10: Hard Questions

1. What hard questions should you be asking in your life? In your organization/company? In your community?

2. What role can you play in answering those questions? What role can you play in making needed change happen? Be specific.

PART 4
LEADERSHIP MATTERS

10

Leadership, Complicit Repercussions and False Security

Healing begins where the wound was made.

—Alice Walker, "The Way Forward Is with a Broken Heart," 2000

After my university's president received a national diversity award, I felt both embarrassed and outraged. I decided to dissect my reasons for dismay via a letter I sent to the university's Black faculty. In the letter, I outlined various racial and gender disparities, put responsibility on the president and the upper administration and called for Black faculty to unite. That letter included the following summary and call to action:

> *In the year before the shooting death of Samuel DuBose, an unarmed Black man stopped off-campus by campus police, the university tripled the number of campus police officers*

and quadrupled the number of stops of Black citizens in just one year. More African-Americans were stopped by the campus police (more than 2,400 in eight months) than Black freshman admitted to the university's main campus in five years.

To be clear, we work at a great institution full of passionate faculty, staff and students. The purpose of this open letter is not to tarnish the university; it is to awaken a sleeping public that has failed to interrogate the actions and the mirage of leadership. If we fail to interrogate the system, we will also fail to interrogate the merits and accolades bestowed in the name of diversity and inclusion. We all play a role. Our complicit silence helps fuel the spiritual and physical demise of other minorities. People of color have lost their lives, careers and mental wellbeing. As one new faculty member wrote to me:

As a result of the way I experience the implicit and explicit race issue on this campus, I decided to take a year leave. After experiencing so many micro and macro aggressions, I needed a break. The psychological results from such treatment leave many faculty, staff and students of color in a bad place. We question the validity of ourselves and our research. I say this in hopes this group can change it or at least provide support for our wounded as they traverse the boundaries of what should not be but has become a battlefield. It is my hope this group can enlighten the lightfaces cloaked in the darkness of bigotry and prejudice. Why are the darkest bodies, the complexioned others, the ones with the most insight? I hope this group can help the university progress. I will be away for this year getting "it" back.

So today, I am making a public promise that I will no longer question my validity of self, research and being. I will interrogate the actions and polices that impact people of color at this university every day. We must not settle for a modest faculty senate resolution that promises more committee meetings and six new "urban" faculty lines. I can no longer pretend as more Black scholars, administrators and professionals leave the university or are treated like second-class citizens. Despite my fears and reluctance to write this, the carnage has not stopped. However, my collective experiences and the psychological warfare waged against me have produced a numbing effect on both the dangers and threats. That has given way to a new form of courageous activism that demands personal sacrifice. We will stand together, or we will continue to fall, one by one.

As soon as I hit the send button, I understood the repercussions of my actions. I knew the administration, the president, my supervisor and other colleagues would read the letter, some in horror, some in elation. I wish I could say I desired either response. I didn't. My letter was not an act of aggression; it was a call to action. While many focused on the negative comments about the university, very few recognized the personal indictment of myself and my complicity in maintaining the status quo. It was easier to accept I was angry at the president and university leadership and to pretend that anger drove my decision to write the letter. But that was not the truth. I had taken a deep and contemplative look at my own failures because I was the administration. I was a part of the university leadership team. I was the community. I was the Black man driving without a front license plate who was shot in the head. I was outraged. This was personal.

I ended the letter with a personal promise to end my complicit silence. It was also a reminder that I had to stop TENDing and Mammying if I wanted to feel truly safe. To be honest, I never felt safe in silence. My silence only generated more fear. And so, the moment I sent the letter was, in fact, the safest moment I had experienced in years.

Most colleagues thought I had gone crazy. Some called me courageous. Truthfully, both are probably accurate, but I was much more comfortable with being called crazy. Courageous felt deceitful. The word courageous made it seem like my message was an act of heroism or that I was acting like a fearless protagonist. That was simply not the case. I was neither a heroine nor was I fearless. I was, in a word, ENRAGED. I had watched the physical, mental and spiritual destruction of my colleagues and friends and RAGE was the only emotion I felt.

A few days after sending the letter, a few Black faculty members felt the need to silence my protest and provide "wise" counsel. For many, this kind of reckless behavior was neither welcomed nor warranted. When they approached me, I turned the table and began asking dangerous questions:

> *"Are you upset by the accuracy of the data in the letter, or that I wrote the letter? Were you aware of the disparate conditions that affected African-American faculty, staff and students at our university? What would have been a*

better response or course of action to address the mounting data that was presented in the letter?"

While no one was prepared to answer these questions, I must say that I was equally unprepared for the minimal response by the Black faculty organization. Outside of a few calls, the organization never made an official statement about the data I highlighted. I assumed they thought the letter was my personal attempt at fame and that I should have remained *quiet when I was serving others or that the room should have felt empty when I was in it.*

No, not this time. I had seen too much. Felt too much. My friend and mentor had died. I had witnessed the personal and professional destruction of countless Black and Brown faculty and staff. His death changed me. It changed the way I viewed the university, diversity and inclusion, and more importantly, it forced to me to take an introspective view into my own personal responsibility. In that moment, I vowed to no longer be a muted bystander.

Months after writing the letter, my former boss confronted me regarding my actions and the impact it had on the university community. She explained how the letter had been seen as an effort to thwart the many efforts and progress the university had made. She felt the letter was a personal attack on her sincere efforts to uphold important values and principles and to advocate for creating a more diverse and inclusive university. She wanted me to understand how my letter and harsh critique had hurt others at the university.

This was a particularly interesting conversation since I had developed, managed and overseen many of the diversity and inclusion accomplishments myself. In fact, my achievements had been highlighted by the president in several speeches and publications, and I was recognized in *The Journal of Blacks in Education*. To suggest that I had written a letter to dismantle the work of diversity and inclusion at the university was simply untrue. It was just the opposite. I was demanding that we do better because I believed we could. As James Baldwin said, "I love America more than any other country in this world, and, exactly for this reason, I insist on the right to criticize her perpetually."[4]

In America, the institution of higher education is the epicenter of knowledge production, public and social research, the intellectual hope for social and economic advancement, and the ceremonious establishment for which democratic citizenry is indoctrinated. For many, formal education and educational equity represent the foundation of freedom--a viable solution to ending all types of oppression, including, but not limited to, race, gender, class, and sex. While this might sound a bit melodramatic to some, as a poor Black girl who has witnessed firsthand the transformative impact of education, I can truly say that I loved my institution and the value that diversity and inclusion practices have in the lives and the social fabric of our democracy. This is why I demanded more, advocated for more and, yes, agitated for more.

As the lengthy conversation with my former boss ended, she searched for an explanation or, better yet, an apology for my actions. I moved slowly to the edge of my seat and said, in sheer indignation, "Our university was involved in killing a man. Given all the facts in the letter, as a Black woman, I'm not sure I could avoid writing it." I said that if people were more concerned about my writing the letter

4 James Baldwin, *Notes of a Native Son* (Boston, MA: Beacon, 1955).

than the serious context or nature of the data it included, then I no longer feared going to lunch alone, being ostracized or being called the angry Black woman. I no longer felt guilty or worried about my actions. Truth be told, what gave me the right to fear losing a job when another human being had lost his life? Not to be self-righteous, but when death and destruction are ever-present, you stop fearing that which seems inevitable. Unfortunately, for me, I had seen too much death and too much destruction. Once again, I rejected the notion of exceptionalism and fully understood how my personal security was dependent upon the survival of other Black and brown bodies. In that moment, I knew my years of avoiding being called the angry Black woman were over. I was angry—and it was time to be completely free.

So I wrote the following "Thought of the Day."

Thought of the Day

> *Starting today, I no longer wish to pretend, or to allow the words "angry Black woman" to stifle my response to oppressive behaviors. I have seen too much and been talked over, talked to and talked around for far too long not to be angry. Today, I wear the badge of angry Black woman proudly, for it reduces the consuming energy of pretense that leads to what William Smith refers to as racial battle fatigue, the side effects of social-psychological or emotional withdrawal, escapism and verbal and nonverbal combativeness.*
>
> *The truth is I express anger at times. I also express happiness, sorrow and complete joy. I don't hear anyone*

saying, "Look at the joyous Black woman walking down the hall." Owning one characteristic—anger—gives me permission to own other ones, such as helpfulness, intuitiveness, spirituality, joyousness, wit and brilliance. It is counterintuitive to spend 80 percent of my time trying not to be labeled angry and only 20 percent of my time working on developing my other traits. Because no matter how "kind, smart or important" I might think I am, to borrow the phrase from the book "The Help" by Kathryn Stockett, my attempts at personal and professional advocacy either on behalf of others or myself can and most often will be interpreted as anger.

So I offer some friendly advice to my former, current and future colleagues across the world who dislike, loathe or admonish my angry Black womanhood—treat me like an equal and know that my RAGE comes from a place of sacrifice and humility. It is the manifestation of my heart crying. For without RAGE, Courage is a fabricated idea.

Journal Entry #11: Thought of the Day

1. Write your own "Thought of the Day."

11

CouRage--When Action Is the Only Option

Not a path for the faint of heart, not but for those who cannot lie any longer. And for those who have no other choice but to live.

—Jeff Foster, "The Way of Rest," 2016

After sending the letter to the Black faculty, I learned that courage is not simply an act of protest against injustice; sometimes, it's believing that the more dangerous path is the only one that produces life. I also believe that real *courage* requires a level of *rage*. Only in times of indignation, or when we are enraged about a particular injustice or action, do we reduce our reliance on the cost-benefit analysis of our own safety or survival.

To put it another way, my Black woman anger had produced courage, and courage is about community. My heartfelt rage for the community and my role in that community produced my courage. This entire experience taught me that leadership is never about individual actions.

It is about how individual actions, or inaction, impact the collective community.

With that in mind, I started questioning why educational leaders seem to carefully evade public dialogues or avoid tackling critical issues around race, gender or discrimination. I wondered why issues such as university policing policies, punitive immigration laws, racial profiling or antiquated tenure policies were not openly discussed or critiqued. I wondered why university officials lacked introspection regarding their own climate of oppression of "others." These are serious questions that warrant serious public debate. And while I wondered out loud, it wasn't until I took part in a university-sponsored training called the Op-Ed Project that I fully understood the dangers of being a public thought leader.

The Op-Ed Project, a national organization established to increase the number of women and underrepresented minorities showcased in the media, came to the university for two years, and I participated in 2015, the second year's training.

As a participant in the program, I wrote and published two articles. The first focused on justice and police brutality in the Black community, and the second examined segregation in diverse communities. The piece about segregation in local communities sparked a visceral reaction I would never have imagined.

In my opinion piece, I highlighted a successful community effort I created to start conscious dialogues about community segregation and the limited presence of diversity in local spaces as well as to create intentional social, economic and civic connections that led to inclusion. The effort was essentially about building community. The article concluded by encouraging others to find proactive ways to create inclusive environments for everyone.

To be clear, the program was not directly connected to the university. However, as a prominent leader in the community, I was known for my advocacy work in the areas of diversity and inclusion and employee recruitment. I had served on several nonprofit boards and a myriad of diversity and inclusion committees that examined recruitment and retention of minority talent both at the university and in local businesses. So it was not a stretch that I would be involved in finding viable solutions to address community segregation.

Equally important to note, my functional role at the university was to increase the recruitment and retention of minority faculty. I launched several programs designed to create inclusive work environments, served on the President's Diversity Council and led university-wide diversity and inclusion efforts.

On the surface, the op-ed seemed neutral, yet once it was in the public domain, the topic turned political as local citizens directly attacked my thoughts and opinions, eventually threatening my position at the university. I was initially shocked by the intense responses, both positive and negative. In a matter of minutes, my words and experiences were dissected as if I, the lauded community leader, was a divisive oddity. Prior to writing the article, I never considered my position would be threatened for expressing my personal experiences and, more importantly, for finding a viable solution to end community isolation. I was certainly naive about the power of my voice. that is, until I received call a from the mayor's office, my immediate supervisor, and a flood of derogatory remarks hit the comments section in the local newspaper. Comments included:

This has to [be] one of the most ignorant editorials of the last couple of years. It's very simple—if you don't see the type of people you want to see, it's because they don't want to be there or they can't afford it! You have an agenda, Ms. Martin! It's so sad that the university includes you in their hypocrisy!

This is such a boatload of tripe! I certainly think less of the university knowing they employ people like Ms. Martin.

The above comments tangled the university's reputation, my individual thoughts and community actions, as if we shared a monolithic existence.

Other comments directly attacked my employment:

Educated folks like Ms. Martin and Mr. Professor have made careers of stirring the racial pot, imagining (or accusing) offenses where none exist. They keep us fighting with each other to keep themselves relevant.

Glad my days of borrowing money to go to school are long gone. Those of you that are borrowing or paying your own way—educational services consumers (students and parents) maybe should be asking the question as to what these vaguely defined positions are bringing to the table and why do you need to borrow money to fund them.

Believe it or not, a thought that came to me was totally unrelated to the thrust of this op-ed piece that the writer has put forth. In this era of sky-rocketing tuition costs and

> *expanding student debt load, one has to think just what is the over-head management cost at this university. As an alum, I always thought the management/ administrative staff was bloated thirty-five plus years ago, but for the life of me I can't determine the role of "...associate provost of special initiatives." Is the mission of this position part of the core mission of the university meaning education? Have things changed that much?*

The comments included thinly veiled threats about my functional role at the university and negated my personal experience and, more importantly, suggested that educational leaders are situated in protected environments, preventing them from knowing the "truth" of local realities. As one person wrote:

> *Or maybe she's just an ivory tower progressive drone spewing the false narrative to keep people like you looking at the wrong hand.*

The entire experience uncovered the dangers, rewards and consequential impact of being a thought leader. I learned that universities and colleges are microcosms of their local and state communities and that dominant cultural beliefs are reflected in that community. I also discovered that any counter-narrative or oppressing viewpoints are unwelcomed and viewed as a threat.

Instead of focusing on my message of building inclusivity, readers attacked me personally, a classic technique to avoid addressing the impact of segregation on communities. This particular experience was different from writing in scholarly journals where academic communities appear to be more civil at a minimum, in part because future research often relies on collective discourse, shared epistemologies and the lauded promotion and tenure process. Writing for the public ripped the safety net off, allowing critics to forego any semblance of collegial decorum, which heightened my fears and triggered personal threats.

The response to the op-ed led me to believe that fear is the preferred tool of oppression. Fear of getting another job, not getting tenure, or being viewed as an outcast often stifles leaders from asking critical questions or tackling difficult issues. To be clear, fears of job security, reduced promotion opportunities and longevity are not new social concerns, nor are they specific to educators. However, in a society that espouses the ideology of meritocracy and the importance of intellectual rigor and democracy, one must wonder why the seemingly "most educated" remain cautious in contributing years of evidence-based research, data and educated opinions on matters that impact the larger society, both inside and outside of scholarly outlets.

Over the past 20 years, I've witnessed an ever-growing undereducated populace and a widening of opportunity gaps—as in opportunities to deliver equitable access to education along racial and economic classes in the United States. These sobering facts remind me that more than ever, there is a great need for public intellectuals, researchers and scholars to analyze, critique and intelligently contribute to the vast national dialogues that impact society.

I've come to believe that in the field of leadership, as we've spent too much time focused on the meaning of leadership, special attributes and power dynamics, we've managed to make highly functioning, emotionally astute introverts feel like they shouldn't have a place at the table. We've managed to make everyone believe that leadership and leading are reserved for a small few. I've come to believe otherwise. Our democracy depends on academia and educational leaders to find ways to vigorously support public intellectuals. Let's face it—educational leaders face serious challenges and dangers, both seen and unseen, from opposing colleagues, university officials, and academic and public stakeholders. However, silence is equally dangerous, especially from those who possess the intellectual capacity to contribute in meaningful ways. The cost of silence is too high, and the impact is long-lasting.

Journal Entry #12: Be Courageous

1. Describe a time in your life when you pushed beyond fear and responded with courage. Be specific. How did this moment change you? How did it change others?

2. Complete the following sentence: I can lead with more courage in the following areas…

12

Ubuntu--All Matters Matter

There is a word in South Africa—Ubuntu—a word that captures [Nelson] Mandela's greatest gift: his recognition that we are all bound together in ways that are invisible to the eye; that there is a oneness to humanity; that we achieve ourselves by sharing ourselves with others, and caring for those around us.

—President Barack Obama, Nelson Mandela memorial, December 10, 2013

Leadership is one of the most observed but least understood social phenomena. While the concept of leader can be traced back to ancient Egyptian rulers, Greek heroes and biblical patriarchs, the study of leadership as an organizational and psychological science has been around for only about 200 years[5].

5 J. M. Burns, *Leadership* (New York: Harper & Row, 1978).

The word leadership means different things to different people. As many scholars have pointed out, there is no single definition of leadership, nor are there research techniques or perspectives broad enough to encapsulate its various aspects[6]. Stogdill[7] stated that there are almost as many definitions of leadership as there are people who have attempted to define it. And as the number of leadership studies, articles, books and self-help manuals has grown, leadership definitions continue to leave many scholars both intrigued and perplexed[8],[9].

Throughout my academic career and my studies in the field of educational leadership, I've read hundreds of books on leadership and leading. Along the way, I began to ask more questions and dig deeper into understanding my own way of knowing the world and concept of leadership. My insatiable desire to connect leadership to my beliefs—that individuals are inextricably linked to one another and that leadership is about relationships and community, not a set of specific behaviors or traits—is what led me to the African philosophy of Ubuntu.

Ubuntu

Ubuntu means: "I am because you are, and you are because I am." It centers on leading in a humanistic way and emphasizes community, collective solidarity and human interdependence.

---

6 T. A. Razik and A. D. Swanson, *Fundamental Concepts of Educational Leadership & Management*, third edition. (Boston, MA: Pearson Education, 2010).

7 R. M. Stogdill, *Handbook of Leadership: A survey of the literature* (New York: Free Press, 1974).

8 K. Leithwood, D. Jantzi, & R. Steinbach, *Changing Leadership for Changing Times* (Buckingham, UK: Open University Press, 1999).

9 G. A. Yukl, G. A., *Leadership in Organizations*, seventh edition (Upper Saddle River, NJ: Prentice Hall, 2010).

Its principles and teachings date back to the first African Homo sapiens, who used the ideas of Ubuntu to settle disputes and conflicts.[10] Known and practiced widely by Africans, the term Ubuntu is derived from the Bantu Nguni language spoken by the Zulu, Xhosa, Swati and Ndebele people. The word Ubuntu means "humanness" or "humanity to others.[11]" It is a cultural and philosophical perspective that espouses the oneness of being human.

Ubuntu embodies five core principles: caring for one another's well-being in a spirit of mutual support; honoring the humanistic value of every individual and acknowledging that leadership cannot exist without actively involving humans; recognizing leadership as a way of life; incorporating the principle of servant leadership; and viewing leadership as a means to secure economic, social and environmental sustainability.[12]

Ncube[7] outlined six core characteristics or behaviors seen in leaders who espouse Ubuntu principles: modeling the way; communal enterprise and shared vision; change and transformation; interconnectedness, interdependency and empowerment; collectivism and solidarity; and continuous integrated development. These six core concepts encompass the social, spiritual and interdependent nature of Ubuntu.

---

10 Dani W. Nabudere, "Ubuntu philosophy: memory and reconciliation," *Texas Scholar Works* (2005): 1–20.

11 L.B.Ncube,"Ubuntu: A transformative leadership philosophy," *Journal of Leadership Studies*, 4 no. 3 (2010): 77– 82.

12 L.Karsten & H. Illa, "Ubuntu as a key African management concept: Contextual background and practical insights for knowledge application," *Journal of Managerial Psychology* 20 no. 7 (2005): 607–20.

Modeling the Way (Esther)

The Ubuntu principle *Modeling the Way* requires leaders to set good examples in their behavior, morals and ethical conduct. Personal traits—such as honesty, sincerity, truthfulness, compassion, empathy, dignity and respect—increase a leader's personal influence within the community.[13] It is only by committing to personal ethical behavior and self-management that people become empowered on both personal and community levels. *Modeling the Way* transcends individual actions or behaviors; it is steeped in the idea that individual actions and responsibilities impact the larger community.

Many of the stories throughout this book symbolize my deep-rooted desire to set good moral and ethical examples. They include my struggle to advance Title IX and resolve pay inequities, speaking out against racial and gender disparities, taking a stance against the belief in Black exceptionalism and embracing and reflecting on my professional and personal mishaps both as a leader and follower. These narratives epitomize what I call my "Esther" moments, times that demanded both individual and global accountability, no matter how difficult. For just like Esther, anyone can sit on the sidelines and forgo their individual responsibility; however, only by forgoing our personal needs and *modeling the way,* can we transform both ourselves and the lives of others. This principle affirms my personal belief that we have *all come to this royal place for such a time as this.*

---

13 C. Malunga, *Understanding Organizational Leadership through Ubuntu* (London: Adonis & Abbey, 2009).

Continuous Integrated Development (Questioning/Self Advocacy)

Starting from within, the Ubuntu principle of *Continuous Integrated Development* demands leaders pursue higher levels of self-awareness and personal growth. In this process, leaders affirm their personal intrinsic values, their limitations and their dependence on others. They understand that their internal struggle toward personal awareness helps transform other individuals, organizations and global outcomes.

My entire journey of self-discovery—from the art of questioning to embracing the way I view leadership—resonates with Ubuntu's core value of *Continuous Integrated Development.* There are numerous examples of my insatiable desire to pursue a deeper level of self-awareness and reflective practice in my accounts of leadership. Examples include how I had to overcome my fear of being great and learn how to compete, how I interrogated my actions or inactions as the associate provost of diversity and inclusion, and how I confronted my own expectations and experiences during and after Hurricane Katrina, to name a few.

Through these experiences, I learned that the principle of *Continuous Integrated Development* extends beyond self-reflective practices and fine-tuning the art of questioning. It is not about finding the "right" answers, but rather is focused on sparking innovations that transform individuals, organizations and communities. For as we gain a better understanding of our individual value, strengths and weaknesses, only then, can we tap into developing the potential of others.

Communal Enterprise and a Shared Vision (Diversity and Inclusion)

The principle of *Communal Enterprises and Shared Vision* in Ubuntu requires that leaders motivate others to share in mutual agreements from which ideas and outcomes are devised to improve the group's social, economic and spiritual outcomes. Maintaining tolerance and a respect for differences while adhering to principles of mutuality remind leaders of their shared humanity.[14] Leaders, then, value others' needs over their own and embrace a core concept that makes room for cross-cultural differences, breaks down hierarchical barriers between leaders and followers and fosters caring communities. Communal decision-making and visioning processes are circular and inclusive; they allow for diverse perspectives and non-monolithic viewpoints.

My career in intercollegiate athletics and as a diversity-and-inclusion thought leader has taught me the imperative value of identifying common goals, articulating a shared vision and incorporating diverse talents and ideas in order to build community. This core principle of Ubuntu can be seen throughout several of the narratives related to diversity and inclusion, my experiences as a senior woman administrator and my actions to confront injustices in both my personal life and professional career. These narratives underscore my belief in the power of true inclusion, in which more voices, creative ideas and new perspectives are not simply allowed at the table but rather incorporated into the very fabric of our individual codes of conduct and institutional practices. For throughout my entire career,

---

14 Corné J. Bekker, "Dreaming with Open Eyes: Reflections on Leadership and Spirituality" (2007), accessedJanuary 9, 2018, https://www.regent.edu/acad/global/publications/working/Dreaming%20with%20Open%20Eyes%20-%20Reflections%20on%20Leadership%20and%20Spirituality%20-%20Bekker%202007.pdf

I learned that the belief in exceptionalism often results in prejudicial actions and thoughts, fear, discrimination and exclusionary practices.

Change and Transformation (Leadership)

The core value of *Change and Transformation* in Ubuntu encourages leaders to search for opportunities to change and transform organizations through people, not of people. More than simple managerial interactions, *Change and Transformation* is entrenched in the ways people interact and share experiences both in and outside of organizations.

As a transformative concept, Ubuntu is much more than a theory for building relationships among leaders and subordinates to maximize personal and organizational goals. It also promotes open conversations, storytelling, inclusive decision-making and participatory communications, all of which transform organizations, people and global systems.

The concept of *Change and Transformation* is a central theme that connects each narrative in this book. Whether I was "Slapping Becky" or fighting for social justice, whether I was changing my personal leadership style to create an inclusive environment or pleading with other educational leaders to become louder public thought leaders, my stories represent more than a rhetorical strategy to convey my personal experiences. They also represent useful tools to encourage, engage and evoke change beyond any single person's limited sphere of influence.

Interconnectedness, Interdependency and Empowerment (Community)

The core principle of Ubuntu, as I keep emphasizing, is human *Interconnectedness and Interdependency*. In Ubuntu, the survival of each individual is literally interdependent upon others. In modern leadership terms, this type of relationship-building is called networking, and its goal is to expand personal, not communal, power.

The Ubuntu perspective purports that *Interconnectedness and Interdependency* thrive in atmospheres where there is trust, collaboration and self-empowerment[15]. Leaders who follow these principles recognize that their individual power and influence come, not from themselves, but from their followers. This revolutionary shift in the power dynamics of leadership requires leaders to adhere to a dependence on followers, not vice versa.

Understanding leadership and leading through the lens of Ubuntu is rooted in the way I view both my individual experiences and my personal responsibilities. This powerful philosophy shifts the emphasis from a single, all-powerful leader to an interconnected community of leaders and followers with shared responsibilities. It is, in the end, the sole premise of this book.

Collectivism and Solidarity (Courage)

In Ubuntu, *Collectivism and Solidarity* underscore the interconnectedness and interdependency of the whole. This core principle espouses the idea that the needs of the collective community

---

15 Ncube, L. B., "Ubuntu: A transformative leadership philosophy," *Journal of Leadership Studies*, 4 no. 3 (2010): 77–82.

are greater than those of individual leaders. This collectivist mentality promotes a spirit of working together toward common organizational and universal goals and shifting from an individual leadership model to a group consensus approach.

The ideas of collectivism and solidarity might sound a bit utopian; however, my experiences in athletics and as a diversity leader have demonstrated time and time again that change and transformation within any organization cannot be sustained without group consensus. As a result, many of my narratives highlight a direct critique of the ideas of meritocracy as a viable solution for economic, political and social parity, for both individuals and our society.

Ubuntu reminds me that there is no single act of leading or leadership that doesn't demand personal introspection and continuous understanding of our individual and collective roles in solving problems. We must aspire to model the way for others, understanding both the enormous burden and gift of that responsibility. We must begin to critically rethink the ideology of meritocracy as individualistic heroism. For over time, my personal experiences and my belief in the humanistic values of Ubuntu have taught me that all matters matter, and that people, organizations, communities and stories are connected. This connection is both local and universal. It is seemingly insignificant at times, yet significant all the time. That is the essence of Ubuntu—*I am because you are; you are because I am.*

Through these parallels and connections, my aim is not to glorify Ubuntu but to highlight and provide insight into its principles and values as they are reflected in my experiences and my approach to both leadership and community.

Make no mistake—the philosophical teachings of Ubuntu should not be romanticized. Not all African people or tribes accept Ubuntu's teachings and practices. Scholars have rightly pointed out the philosophy's "ubiquitous conflicts and contradictions."[16] Additionally, Ubuntu is not intended to replace Western leadership philosophies, but to add diversity to existing leadership theories by incorporating other traditions and potentially dismantling the ideology of superiority and dominance inherent in some Eurocentric leadership theories. Murtadha and Watts emphasized that "the current ways of examining leadership leave absent the narrative voices and contributions of underrepresented minorities and create a theoretical vacuum which limits the academy's ability to frame problems and produce viable strategies that transform education globally."[17]

Looking back, I see the principles of Ubuntu reflected in my childhood values, guiding my ever-present litany of questions and fueling both my informal and formal education about leadership. The lessons shared throughout this book are, in some ways, cautionary tales as well as bits of wisdom I have gained over the years. Ubuntu is simply how I've come to see, practice and explore the world of leadership. It has helped me approach my work and my life in a broader perspective. It helps explain why I instinctively ask questions and keep my eyes wide open, and why I can't remain silent about critical issues, whether I am seated at the head or the foot of the table. It also explains why I have never accomplished any meaningful task alone, nor will I ever.

---

16 W. M. J. Van Binsbergen, "Ubuntu and the globalisation of southern African thought and society," *Quest: An African Journal of Philosophy* 15, no. ½ (2001): 53–89.

17 K. Murtadha & D. M. Watts, "Linking the struggle for education and social justice: A historical perspective on African American leadership in schools," *Educational Administration Quarterly* 41, no. 4 (2005): 591-608.

Progress and accomplishments always require others, in particular others whose actions are interconnected with mine.

I share these Ubuntu principles in the context of my lived experiences, because my 20-plus-year career in academia has taught me many lessons, but one in particular echoes through generations: We are all connected. Our stories are connected; our actions and inactions are connected. As the African proverb states: “A rooster may belong to one household, but when it crows, it crows for the whole village.”

Therefore, our new call is to do more than care for the least of us, or aspire toward greater diversity or inclusion, or even to do the “right” thing. Our new call is about accepting, questioning and honoring our own humanity, the humanity of others and the collective impact on our local and global communities. With Ubuntu as a guide, I now understand that leadership and leading are, at the core, about community.

Thought of the Day

Courage requires personal sacrifice, a deep love for humanity, and more importantly, the understanding that we are all interconnected. It requires each of us, individually and collectively, to be better and demand better. For we are the change we desperately seek.

Journal Entry #13: Demanding More

1. In what areas of your leadership journey must you demand better of yourself?

2. Outline specific actions and personal commitments you will make starting today.

13

REMEMBERING SELF

So it is only befitting that I end this book with a personal affirmation. For every word, every narrative and every "Thought of the Day" is a part of my individual, and our collective, healing. Together, these narratives recognize, celebrate and examine the struggles, leadership and practical wisdom that Black women have to offer higher education, intercollegiate athletics, and diversity and inclusion. I pray the narratives spark change, restore and challenge the way we examine both our actions or inactions in community.

My greatest hope, however, is that everyone reading this book, especially women of color, who have questioned their intellectual, spiritual, political, cultural or leadership capacity, know that you are not alone and that our journey is magical. For We, the collective WE, are the peace the world awaits. We are the perfect manifestation of our ancestors. We represent their hopes, dreams and the future kingdoms for which we were chosen to rule.

So embrace and take-hold of this magical journey with resilience and courage. *For we have come to this royal place for such a time as this.*

I close this book with a personal affirmation or "Thought of the Day".

> *Blackgirlmagic is real. Ask me how I know, and I'll chant Ubuntu—I am because you are, and you are because I am. For we are the perfect manifestation of our ancestry, representing the hopes, dreams and the future kingdoms for which we were carefully selected to rule. We owe nothing in particular, yet are indebted to those who have come before us, those we currently serve and those who will tend to our remains.*
>
> *Let us never forget that every action produces a reaction, which leads to a consequence. Consequences are inescapable.*
>
> *So journey on, no longer bound by the illusion of place or safety, but rather, by the discovery of how our individual gifts, talents and resources can produce new life for individuals and organizations. We must model the way, transform and change lives, and most importantly, recognize our interdependence on each other. As we have been given, so have we received.*
>
> *Remember, "Those who are born different are the truly privileged ones. For it is our calling to live exceptional lives. While we may damn the weight of the burden, let us also give thanks for the gift."*

Keep your eyes open, ask the tough questions and advocate for yourself and others, even when it feels burdensome and weighty. Especially then. For our paths are courageously built on the backs of our ancestors. It is a voyage we must complete despite the physical, psychological and spiritual anguish we might experience. It will require courage. And in the words of Nelson Mandela: "Courage is not the absence of fear, but triumph over it. The brave man is not he who does not feel afraid, but he who conquers that fear."

No matter how many times they call you the Angry Black Woman, know that our collective survival requires—no demands—our rage, anger and indignation. Embrace your angry Black womanhood or manhood because it produces courage. Courage is not simply an act of protest against normalcy; sometimes it's believing that the more dangerous path is the only one that produces life and freedom.

So don't pretend. Remove the mask and discover the unique person living inside you, for everything we desire lies outside our comfort zone. As Jeff Foster states: "For if it makes you weak, if it scares you, if it takes you to the bleeding edge of your identity, it may just be your true path."

Finally, leadership is hard and not for the faint of heart. It is a journey that produces fear, challenges, loneliness, victories and renewal. It is a dizzying path of vast opportunities. It's the moment we've all been preparing for—our "Esther" moment. Welcome to the journey.

Journal #14: I AM

Starting with the statement, "I AM," narrate your story. In your own words, the statement should include your gifts, your values and your guiding principles. Be generous with yourself.

Here are a few examples:

I AM the one who slapped Becky and fights against social injustices by keeping my eyes-wide open, asking the critical questions that expose the truth, then taking action knowing that I have come for such a time as this…

I AM the peace the world awaits. A determined life force destined for greatness. I AM the curious kid in the back of the room filled with both fear and doubt who finds the courage to ask the difficult questions and act on behalf of humanity. Filled with flaws, I AM on a journey of self-discovery that requires that I understand my privilege, power, place and responsibility to others. For I AM the hopes, dreams and the manifestation of Ms. Gladys' beautiful garden…

I AM

Made in the USA
Middletown, DE
13 June 2023